Windows Me

QUICK FIX

TEACH YOURSELF BOOKS

For UK orders: please contact Bookpoint Ltd, 130 Milton Park, Abingdon, Oxon OX14 4SB. Telephone: (44) 01235 400414, Fax: (44) 01235 400454. Lines are open 9.00 – 6.00, Monday to Saturday, with a 24-hour message answering service. E-mail: orders@bookpoint.co.uk

British Library Cataloguing in Publication Data
A catalogue record for this title is available from the British Library.

First published 2001 by Hodder Headline Plc, 338 Euston Road, London, NW1 3BH.

Typeset by Mac Bride, Southampton
Printed in Great Britain for Hodder & Stoughton Educational, a division of Hodder Headline Plc, 338 Euston Road, London NW1 3BH by Cox & Wyman, Reading, Berkshire.

Impression number 10 9 8 7 6 5 4 3 2 1
Year 2006 2005 2004 2003 2002 2001

Contents

WINDOWS ESSENTIALS

Getting started

Discover the desktop

What do you see when you look at the screen? The answer will depend upon what you are doing and how you have set up your PC, but some or all of these items should be visible.

The *background* may be a flat colour, a pattern, a picture or a Web page. It can be changed at any time (see page 102).

Shortcuts are icons with links to programs, to folders (for storing files on the hard disk) or to Web pages. Click an icon to run its program, open the folder or go into the Internet. There are some shortcuts at the start, and you can add your own (see page 94).

The *Taskbar* is normally present as a strip along the bottom of the screen, though it can be moved elsewhere (see page 141). It is the main control centre for the Desktop, carrying the tools and buttons to start and to switch between applications.

Click the **Start** button to open the *Start menu*. Any program on your PC can be run from here. The menu also leads to recently-used documents, favourite places on the Internet, the Help pages and other utilities.

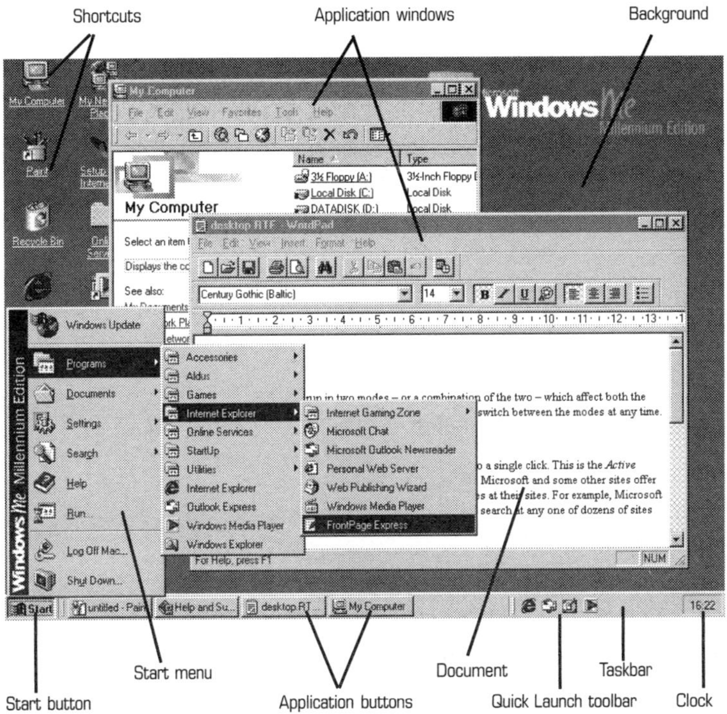
Shortcuts
Application windows
Background
Start button
Start menu
Application buttons
Document
Quick Launch toolbar
Taskbar
Clock

Use the mouse

The mouse is almost essential for work with Windows – you can manage without it, but not as easily. It is used for selecting and manipulating objects, highlighting text, making choices, and clicking icons and buttons – as well as for drawing in graphics applications.

There are five key 'moves'.

Point

Move the mouse so that the tip of the arrow (or the finger of the hand) is over the object you want to point to.

- If you point to an icon, and hold the cursor there for a moment, a label will appear, telling you about the icon.

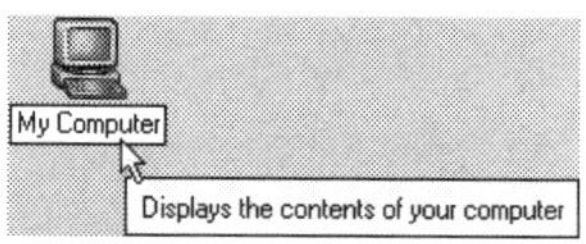

- If you reach the edge of the mouse mat before the pointer has reached its target, pick the mouse up and put it down again in the middle of the mat.

Click

A single click of the left mouse button.

Right-click

A single click of the right mouse button.

Double-click

Two clicks, in quick succession, of the left mouse button. The response of the mouse can be adjusted to suit your double-click speed (see page 126).

Drag

Point to an object or place on the Desktop, hold down the left button and draw the cursor across the screen (see page 33).

Use the keyboard

The keyboard is mainly for entering text, but can also be used for editing text and controlling the system.

These keys are worth identifying and remembering:

Windows – press to open the Start menu. Also used in some keyboard shortcuts.

Control

Control – used in combination with other keys for shortcuts to menu commands.

Alt

Alt – mainly used for menu selections (page 10).

Application – displays the shortcut menu (page 14) of the item that is currently selected.

or Enter **Enter** keys, used after entering text or for selecting.

Esc

Escape – press this to abandon an operation, e.g. when selecting from a menu or after opening a dialog box by mistake.

F1

The first **Function** key. This one always calls up Help. The others do different jobs, depending upon the application.

Tab – moves a set distance (typically 1cm) across the page in a word-processing program, also moves the cursor from one box to the next in data entry forms.

Backspace – deletes the selected object on screen or the letter to the left in a block of text.

Delete – deletes the selected object on screen or the letter to the right in a block of text.

Home End Jump to the top/bottom of a block of text or a window display.

PgUp PgDn Scroll up/down one window length.

↑ ↓ Move through text, menus and folder displays.

← → If you hold down **Control** while pressing these, it usually produces faster movement.

Use a menu

The pop-up Start menu and the pull-down menus in Windows applications are structured and used in the same way.

- If an item has an ▶ on the right, a submenu will open when you point to the item.
- If an item has … after the name, a panel or dialog box (page 16) will open when you point to the item.

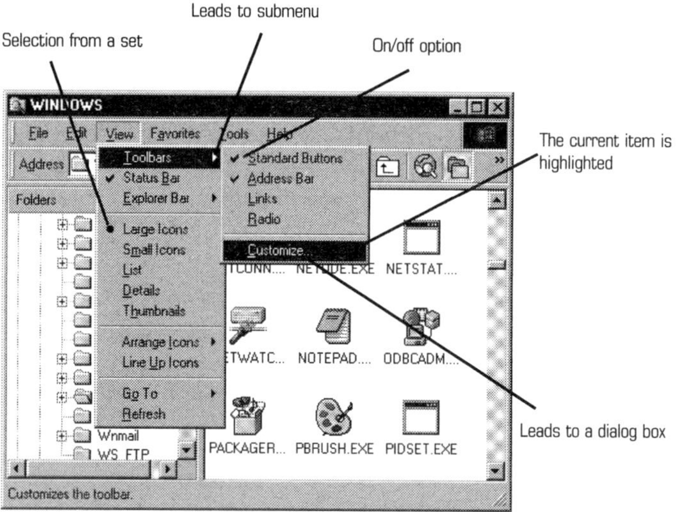

- If an item has ■ to its left, it is the selected option from a set.
- If an item has ✔ to its left, it is an option and is turned on – click to turn it off or on again.
- If a name is in grey ('greyed out'), the command is not available at that time – you probably have to select something first.

Select from a menu with the mouse

- To open the Start menu, click on the **Start** button.
- To open a menu in a program, click on its name in the Menu bar.
- To open a submenu, point to its name.
- To run a command or set an option, click on it.
- To leave the menu system without selecting a command, click anywhere else on the screen.

Select from a menu using keys

Open the menu

1 Press the **Windows** button to open the Start menu.

Or

2 In a program, hold down **Alt** and press the underlined letter in the name on the Menu bar, e.g. **F** to open the File menu.

Select a command

Either

3 Press the underlined letter of the name to run the command, set the on/off option or open the submenu.

or

4 Move through the menus with the arrow keys – up/down the menu and right to open submenus – then press **Enter**.

- The left/right arrows will move you from one menu to the next.
- Press **Escape** to close the menu without selecting a command.

Use keyboard shortcuts

Many applications allow you to run some of the most commonly used commands directly from the keyboard, without touching the menu system. For example, in Paint, **Control + S** (i.e. hold down the **Control** key and press **S**) will call up the **Save** command; **Control + O** has the same effect as selecting **Open** from the **File** menu.

The shortcuts vary, and some applications will offer far more than others, but some are common to all – or most – applications. If a command has a keyboard shortcut, it will be shown on the menu, to the right of the name.

Use smart menus

The Start menu is a *smart* menu! It has been designed to respond to the way you work, displaying at first only the core items and those that you use regularly. The rest are tucked out of sight, but can be revealed either by waiting a few moments or by clicking on the double-arrow bar at the bottom of the menu. If you use a program, it will be added to the menu, and become part of the displayed set in future. If you don't use a program for several days, it will be dropped from the menu.

For example, here's what happened when I last tried to run Media Player.

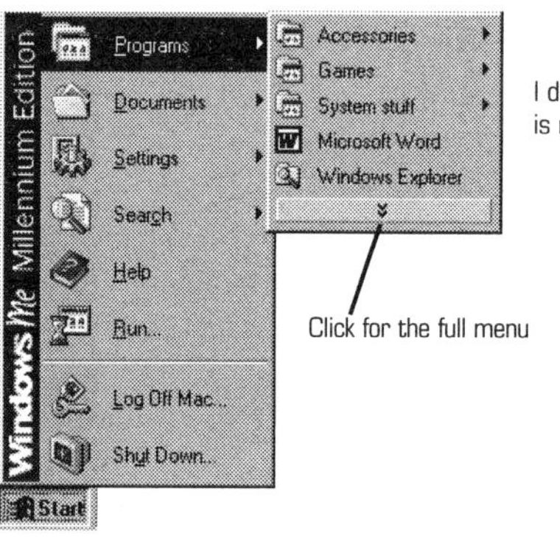

Click for the full menu

I don't use Media Player often, so it is not part of the normal display

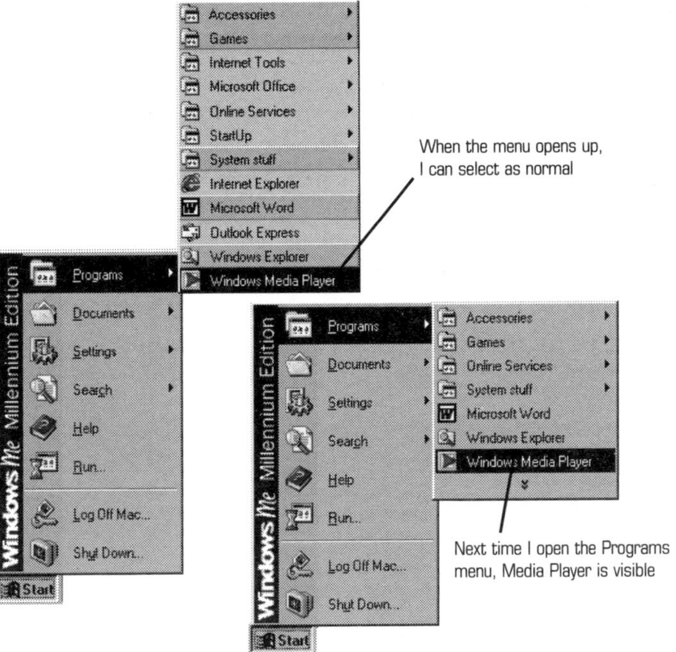

tip

On a new PC, it takes about 10 sessions for the Start menu to get smart.

Use shortcut menus

Shortcut or *context menus* can be opened for more or less anything on the screen – a Desktop icon, the Taskbar or the background, a file or folder in My Computer, a selected object or block of text in a program. This menu will contain a set of commands and options that are relevant to the object in that context.

To open a shortcut menu

1 Right-click on the object.

or

2 If the object is already selected, press the **Application** key.

3 Select from the menu in the usual way.

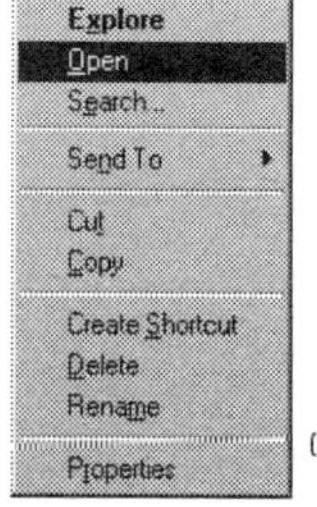

(A)

(B)

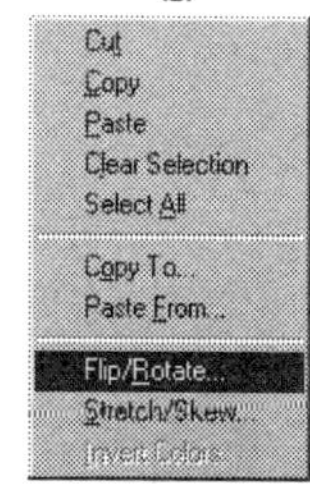

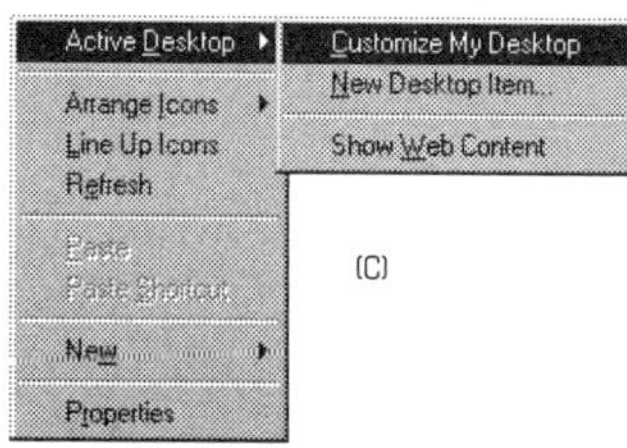

(C)

EXAMPLES OF SHORTCUT MENUS, FROM (A) A FOLDER, (B) A SELECTED AREA IN PAINT AND (C) THE DESKTOP

View properties

Most objects have *Properties*, which define what they look like and how they work. These can be seen and set through the **Properties** panels, which can be reached via the context menus.

Properties panels often have several *tabs*, dealing with different aspects of the object. Some will simply contain information, such as the details of a file; others have options that you can set.

- To switch between tabs, click on the name at the top.

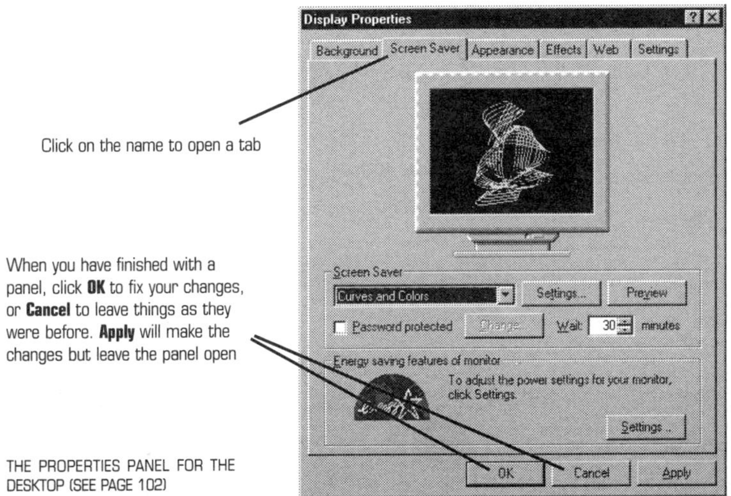

THE PROPERTIES PANEL FOR THE DESKTOP (SEE PAGE 102)

Set options and properties

An object's options can be set in its Properties panel. Within a program, options are set and information given through *dialog boxes*. The same methods are used in panels and dialog boxes.

Text boxes

Used for collecting filenames or other details. Sometimes a value will be suggested by the system. Edit it, or retype it if necessary.

Drop-down lists

Click to drop down

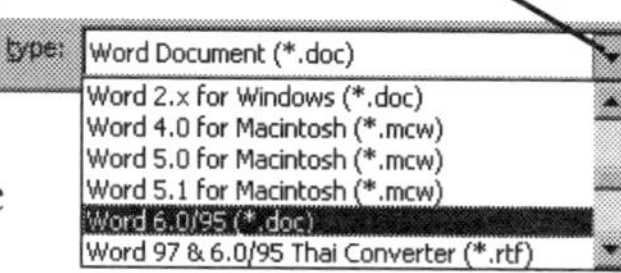

These look like text boxes but with an arrow to the right. Click on the arrow to drop down the list, then select a value.

Lists

With a simple list, just scroll through it and select a value. They sometimes have a linked text box. The selected value is displayed there, but you can also type in a value.

Check boxes

These are switches for options – click to turn them on or off. Check boxes are sometimes found singly, but often in sets. You can have any number of check boxes on at the same time, unlike radio buttons.

Radio buttons

These are used to select one from a set of alternatives. Click on the button or its name to select.

Sliders and number values

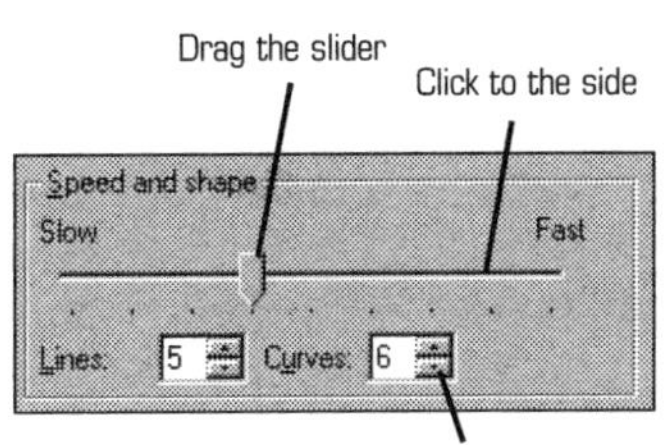

Sliders are used where an approximate value will do – for example, volume control. Drag the slider to increase or decrease, or click to the side of the slider to move it towards the click point.

Numbers are often set through scroll boxes. Click the up or down arrows to adjust the value. If you want to make a big change, type in a new value.

Start a program

All the programs now on your PC, and any that you install later, should have an entry in the **Programs** part of the **Start** menu.

A program may be on the first level of this menu, or may have been grouped onto a submenu – which may open up to a further level of submenus. Windows Me sets the basic structure. The installation routines for new software will create the Start menu entries and organize them into submenus, but if you do not like the structure, you can tailor it to suit yourself (see page 146).

To start a program:

1. Click Start or press [Windows key] on your keyboard.
2. Point to **Programs** with the mouse
3. If the program name is not visible, point to a group name to open the next level of menu – and again if necessary.
4. Click once on a program name.

tip

You can select from the Start (and any other) menu using the keyboard – see page 10).

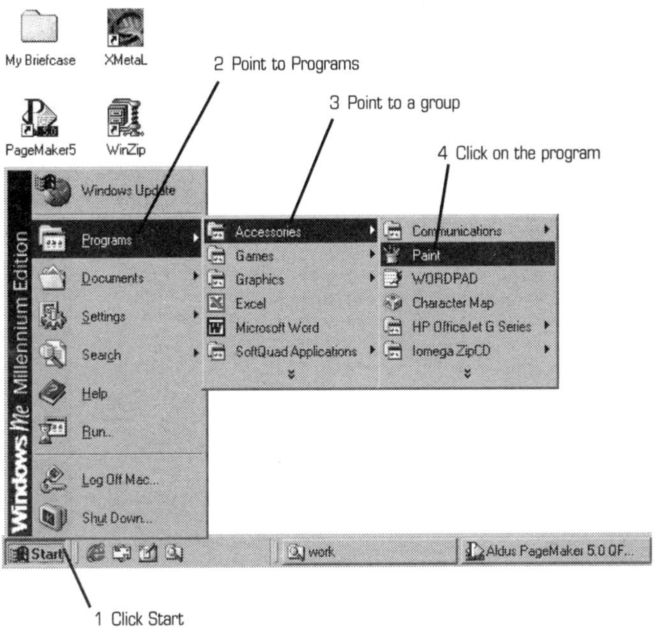

RUNNING A PROGRAM FROM THE START MENU. IN THIS CASE, THE PROGRAM, **PAINT**, IS ON THE SECOND LEVEL OF SUBMENUS

Start from Documents

Those documents that you have been working on recently can be opened from the Documents folder on the Start menu.

1 Click on **Start**.

2 Point to **Documents**. Its submenu has shortcuts to your most recently used documents.

3 Select a document to run the linked application and open the document.

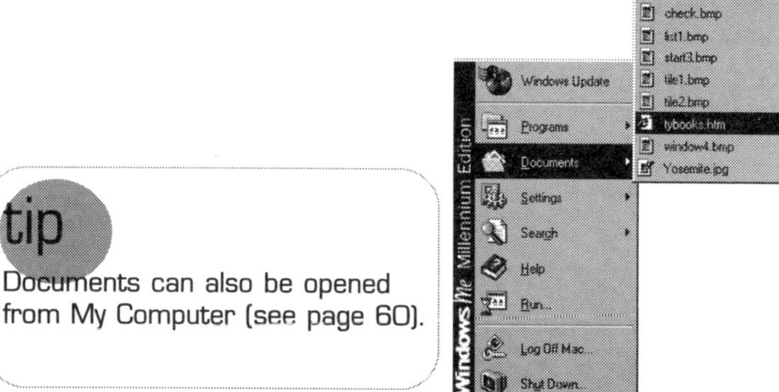

Start from the Desktop

Shortcuts offer a quick route to folders and programs. When you first start using Windows Me, you will find a dozen of these icons on the Desktop. Some, such as My Documents, lead to folders – click on these and My Computer will run, open at the selected folder. Others, such as the Internet Explorer icon, lead to applications – click on these to start the application.

If you want to add shortcuts to favourite applications, it can be done easily through My Computer (see page 94).

tip

Every type of document is linked to an application (see *File Types* on page 68), so that any time you open a document, Windows will run the appropriate application for you.

Start from the Quick Launch toolbar

The Quick Launch toolbar gives you ready access to three of the more commonly used applications: Internet Explorer, Outlook Express and Media Player.

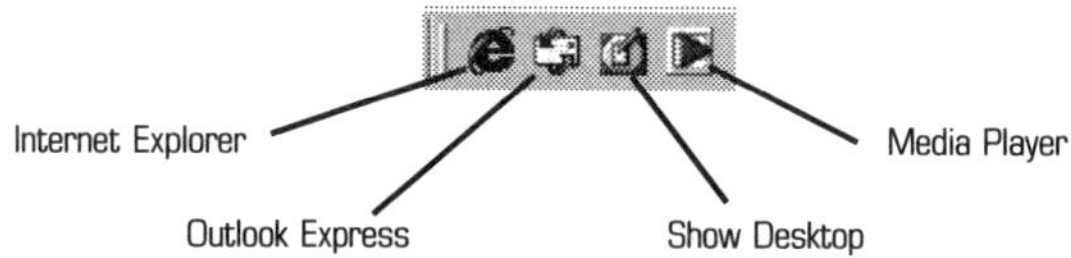

- Click the Show Desktop icon to hide any open windows so that you can see the Desktop.
- Click it again to restore all the hidden windows to view.

You can add shortcuts to the toolbar or create new Taskbar toolbars (see page 138).

See *Quick Fix Internet Explorer 5.5/Outlook Express 5* for more on these applications.

Shut Down

When you have finished a working session, you must shut down the system properly.

1 Click **Start** and select **Shut Down**. If any windows are open, they will be closed. You may be prompted to save documents.

2 Select **Shut Down** and click **OK**.

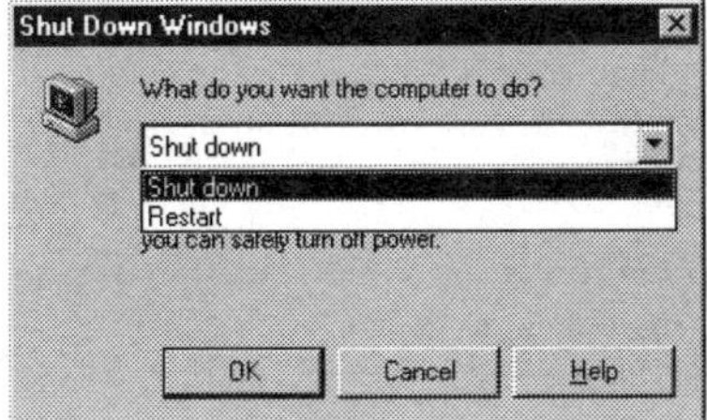

Restart will normally restore order after a crash – see the next page

3 Wait until you are told that it is safe before turning off.

tip

Some PCs have a Suspend mode which shuts down the screen and hard drive, but leaves the memory intact, allowing a very quick startup when you next want to use the PC.

Recover from a crash

Windows Me is quite robust, but software is rarely perfect. Some applications – and some combinations of applications – are more likely than others to crash.

You will know your system has crashed if:

- The busy symbol appears and stays (but do wait twice as long as normal just in case it has a lot more to do than you thought).
- There is no response to key presses or mouse actions.

Crashes are normally caused by two programs trying to use the same area of memory, and you can go find a big technical book if you want to know more about this!

Solution

1 Hold down **Ctrl** and **Alt**, and press **Delete**. The **Close Programs** dialog box will appear, and the program that has crashed will have 'not responding' after the name.

2 If it is an *application* that is not responding, click **End Task** – you will be asked to confirm that you really want to close it. The system should work properly once it is out of the way.

3 If *Explorer* or *Systray* is 'not responding', click **Shut Down** and select **Restart** at the **Shut Down Windows** dialog box. Windows cannot function if these are not working properly.

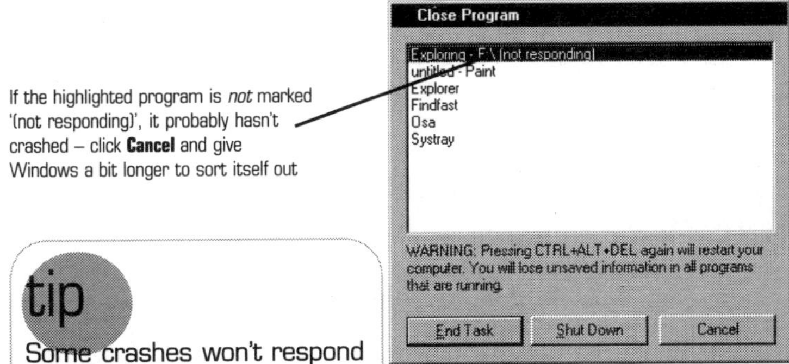

If the highlighted program is *not* marked '(not responding)', it probably hasn't crashed – click **Cancel** and give Windows a bit longer to sort itself out

tip

Some crashes won't respond to this routine. In these cases, just turn the PC off.

Basic techniques

Select text

Before you can do any work on an object or a set of objects – e.g. format a block of text, copy part of an image, move a group of files from one folder to another – you must select it.

Select text with the mouse:

1 Point to the start of the text.
2 Hold down the left mouse button and drag across the screen.
3 The selected text will be highlighted.

Select text with the keyboard:

1 Move the cursor to the start of the text.
2 Hold down the **Shift** key.
3 Use **Home**, **End**, **Page Up**, **Page Down** or the arrow keys to highlight the text you want.

MOUSE
Drag over the area, holding the left button down

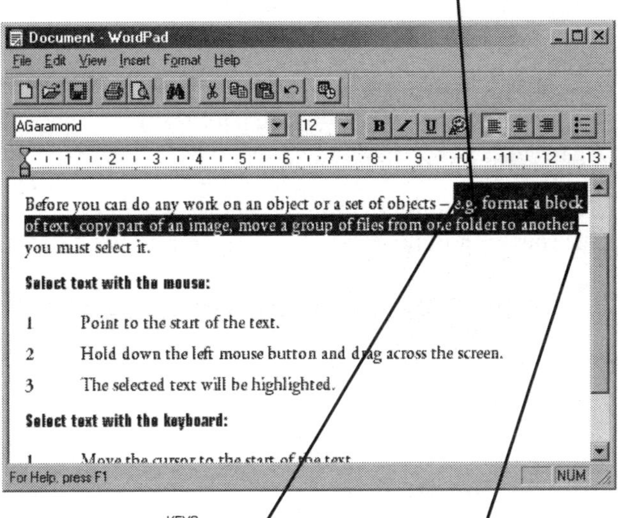

KEYS
Point to the start, hold down **Shift** and move to the end

Select graphics or icons

Single object:

- Point to it. If this does not highlight it, click on it.

Adjacent objects:

1. Imagine a rectangle that will enclose the objects.
2. Point to one corner of this rectangle.
3. Hold down the left mouse button and drag across to the opposite corner – an outline will appear as you do this.

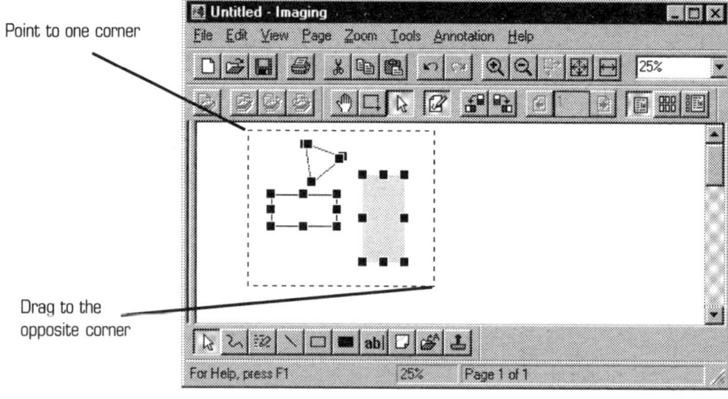

or

4 Select the object at one corner.

5 Hold down **Shift** and select the object at the opposite corner.

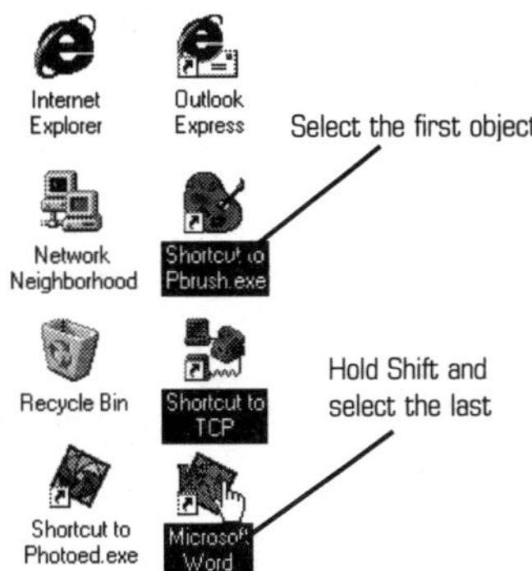

Scattered objects:

1 Highlight the first object.

2 Hold down the **Ctrl** key and highlight each object in turn.

3 If you select an object by mistake, point to (or click on) it again to remove the highlighting.

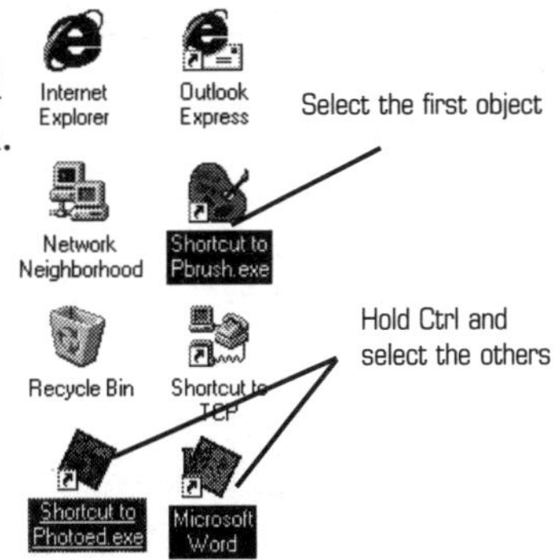

Delete objects or text

The same techniques are used on the Desktop and in programs, and apply to objects and to characters or blocks of text.

1 Select the object(s) or block of text.

2 Right-click for the shortcut menu or – in a program – open the **Edit** menu and select **Delete**.

Or

3 Press the **Delete** or **Backspace** key.

If you delete something by mistake, you can usually recover it either by pressing **Control + Z** or with the **Undo** command on the **Edit** menu.

Cut, Copy and Paste

These can copy and move data within and between applications.

- **Copy** copies a selected block of text, picture, file or other object into a special part of memory called the *Clipboard*.
- **Cut** deletes the data, but places a copy into the Clipboard.
- **Paste** inserts the data into a new place in the same or a different application.

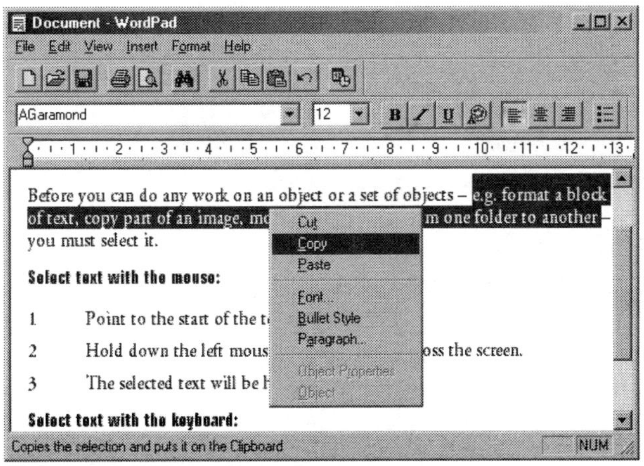

THE SHORT MENU OFFERS THE QUICKEST ROUTE TO THE CUT AND PASTE COMMANDS. IF THE CLIPBOARD IS EMPTY, PASTE WILL BE 'GREYED OUT' OR OMITTED FROM THE MENU

Selected graphics usually have an enclosing frame with 'handles' at the corners and mid-sides. You can drag within the frame to move the object, or on the handles to resize it

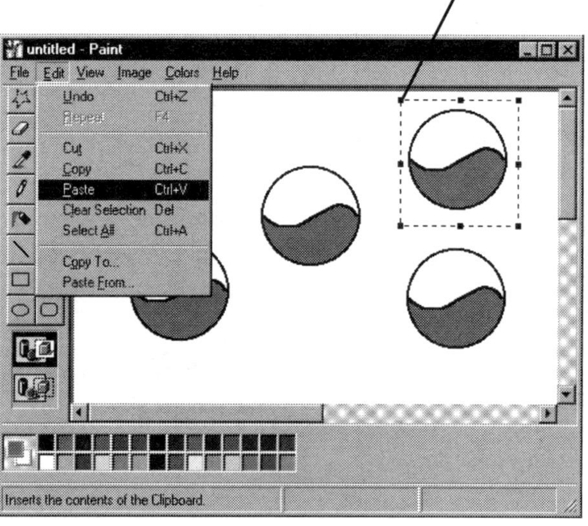

PASTING A COPIED IMAGE IN PAINT – THE SAME DATA CAN BE COPIED AS MANY TIMES AS YOU WANT – AND IN THE SAME OR IN DIFFERENT APPLICATIONS

Drag and drop

Use this for moving objects within or between applications, or for rearranging files and folders (see page 78).

1 Select the block of text or the object(s).

2 Point anywhere within the highlighted text or object.

3 Hold down the mouse button and drag the object across the screen or, with text, move the cursor (which is now).

4 Release the button to drop the object into its new position.

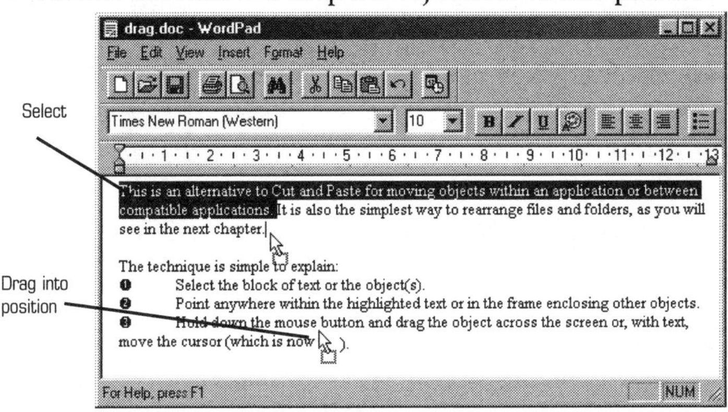

DRAGGING TEXT IN WORDPAD. THE TARGET POSITION FOR THE TEXT IS MARKED BY THE THIN BAR TO THE LEFT OF THE ARROW

Help

Get Help and Support

The main Windows Me Help system is reached through the **Help** item on the **Start** menu.

- Click **Start**, select **Help** and you are in.

It will take a little while to load in – get used to it. Help comes slowly, even on a fast PC!

The Help and Support has four sections. *Home* and *Index* are the two most important of these.

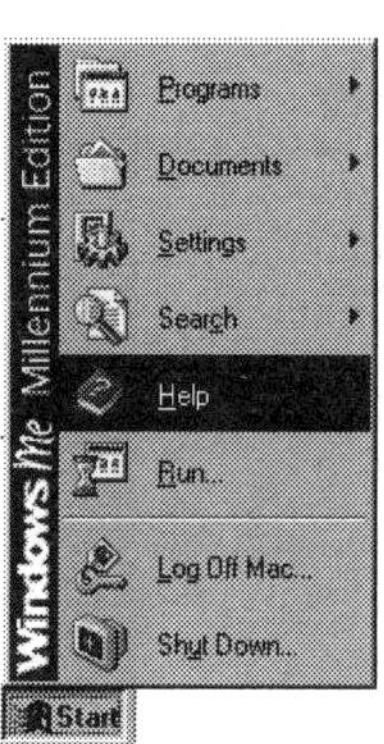

tip

You can also start Windows Help and Support from the Desktop, or get Help within any application, by pressing [F1].

Start from the Home Help

The Home section acts as a contents list, with cross-references, all joined together by hyperlinks. At the top level are a set of major content headings. Click on one of these links to open its page. The links at this level may be to lists of sub-topics, or directly to Help pages (marked by ?) or to Help on the Web (marked by e) or to 'Tours & tutorials' (marked by).

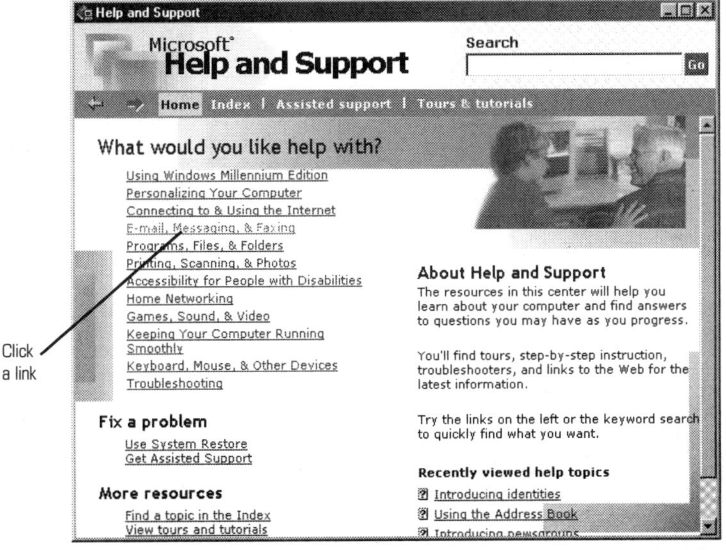

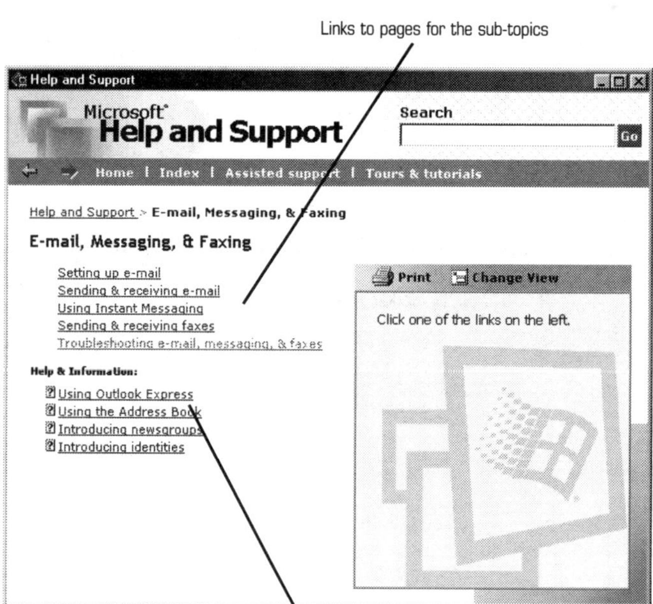

FOLLOWING THE LINKS IN THE HOME SECTION OF HELP AND SUPPORT. ON THIS SECOND-LEVEL PAGE THERE ARE LINKS TO FIVE MORE SUB-TOPICS AND TO FOUR PAGES OF HELP

Use a troubleshooter

The troubleshooters will take you through a series of checks and activities to try to diagnose and cure problems.

1 Work through the contents to find a relevant topic.

2 If there is a troubleshooter listed at the bottom, click on it.

3 Follow the instructions – and they usually work!

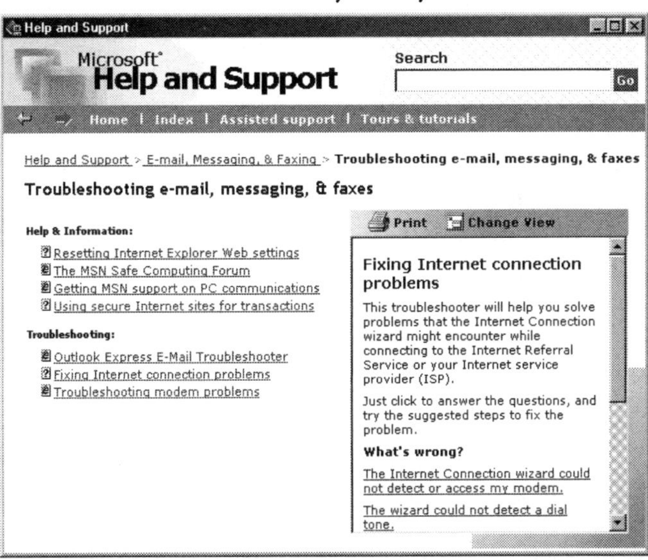

Find Help through the Index

To switch to the Index:

1 Click on the Index label in the menu bar.

2 Drag on the slider or click the down arrow to scroll through the index entries.

or

3 Start to type a keyword in the top box. As you type, the list will scroll to the words that begin with the typed letters.

4 Pick a topic from the list and click Display.

5 If there are several Help pages for the same index entry, you will be offered a choice – pick one and click Display.

The Help pages that you find here are the same as those linked from the Home section.

tip

A 'keyword' is simply any word that describes what it is you are looking for. If a word does not give you what you want, try a different word to describe it.

If you start to type, the list scrolls to those letters

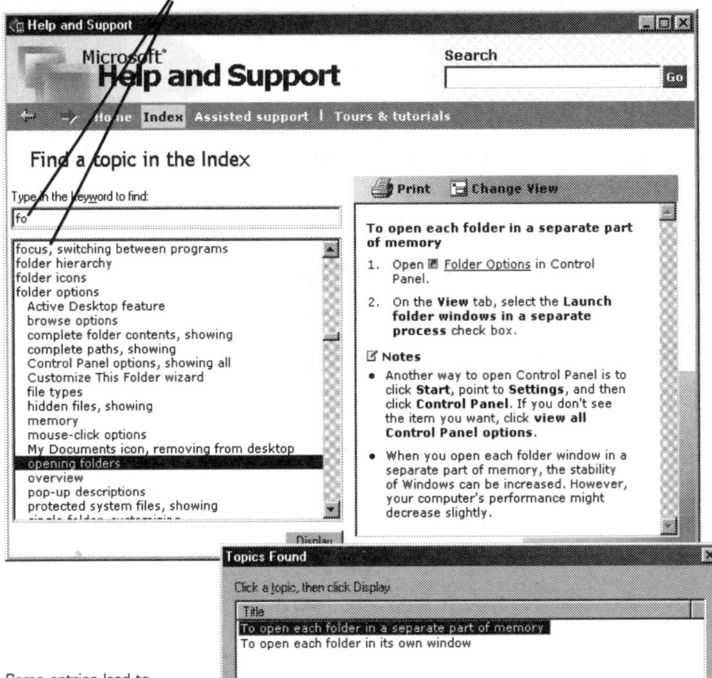

Some entries lead to several topics – pick one and click **Display**

Search for Help

The **Search** box is present on every page of the Help system.

1 To run a search, type your keyword into the box and click **Go**.

2 A list of pages containing your keyword will be displayed on the left of the window – click one to read its Help page.

Type a keyword and click **Go**

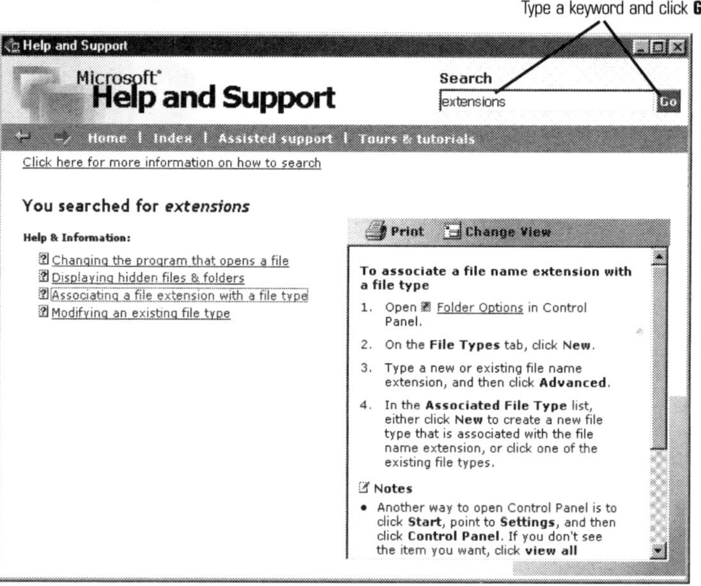

Change the Help View

The **Change View** option shuts down the surrounding Help and Support window and leaves just the topic display. This can be very useful if you want to keep the information visible while you tackle that tricky job.

1 On the header bar of the Help topic, click **Change View**.

2 If necessary, resize the window to show more of the entry – or to make it smaller – and move it to a convenient part of the screen so that you can still read it while working on whatever you needed the Help on.

- Click to reopen the full window when you need it.

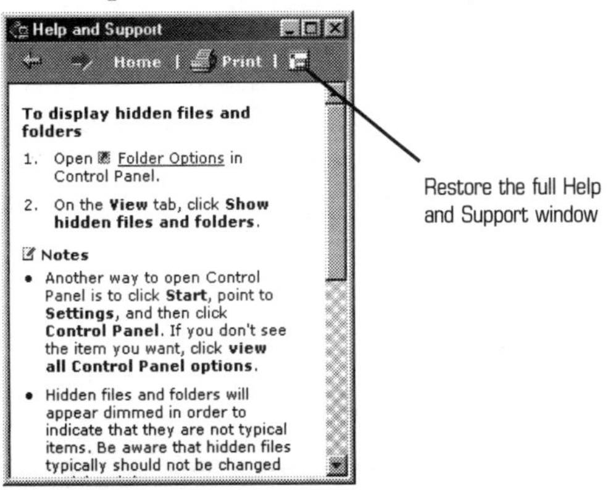

Get support from the Web

If you can't find what you want in the Home or Index sections, go to the **Assisted Support** page to look for online support at Microsoft and MSN.

- The Microsoft link is direct to them;
- The MSN links first display a list of forums and message boards in the topic display area.

Pick one of these and go online.

tip

It takes longer to get Help online, but there is far more available over a far wider range of topics – and you may be able to help others as well.

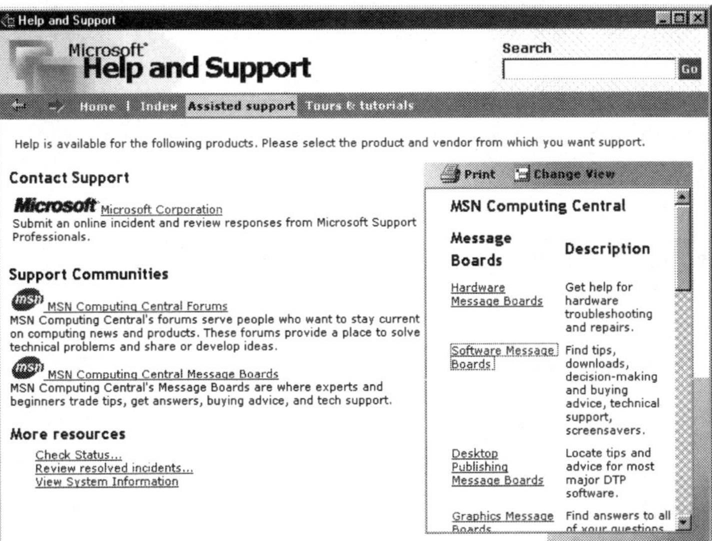

tip

If you read to the bottom of a Help page, you will normally then find links to other similar topics. Some pages will simply have the label '<u>Related topics</u>'. Clicking on this will look up the topic in the Index for you.

USING WINDOWS

Managing windows

Identify the parts

A window is a framed area of the screen that exists independently of any other windows. All applications are displayed in windows. If an application can handle multiple documents, each document is displayed in its own window within the application.

All windows have these features:

- **Title bar** along the top – showing the name of the application or document;
- **Minimize**, **Maximize/Restore** and **Close** buttons on the far right of the title bar – for changing the mode (page 50) and for shutting down;
- An icon at the far left of the Title Bar – leading to the window's **Control menu** (page 51);
- **Scroll bars** along the right and bottom – for moving the contents within the frame. These are only present if the contents are too wide or too long to fit within the frame.
- A thin outer **border** – for changing the size (see page 54).

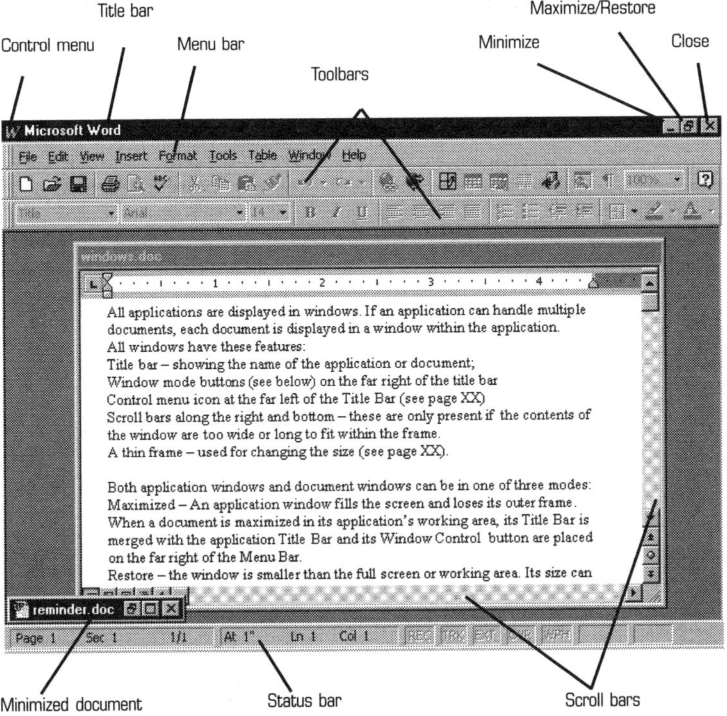
Title bar
Control menu
Menu bar
Toolbars
Maximize/Restore
Minimize
Close
Microsoft Word
File Edit View Insert Format Tools Table Window Help
All applications are displayed in windows. If an application can handle multiple documents, each document is displayed in a window within the application.
All windows have these features:
Title bar – showing the name of the application or document;
Window mode buttons (see below) on the far right of the title bar
Control menu icon at the far left of the Title Bar (see page XX)
Scroll bars along the right and bottom – these are only present if the contents of the window are too wide or long to fit within the frame.
A thin frame – used for changing the size (see page XX).
Both application windows and document windows can be in one of three modes:
Maximized – An application window fills the screen and loses its outer frame. When a document is maximized in its application's working area, its Title Bar is merged with the application Title Bar and its Window Control button are placed on the far right of the Menu Bar.
Restore – the window is smaller than the full screen or working area. Its size can
reminder.doc
Page 1 Sec 1 1/1 At 1" Ln 1 Col 1
Minimized document
Status bar
Scroll bars

Application windows also have:

- **Menu bar** – giving access to the full range of commands and options;
- One or more **Toolbars** – containing icons that call up the more commonly used commands and options. Toolbars are normally along the top of the working area, but may be down either side, or as 'floating' panels anywhere on screen.
- The **Status bar** – displaying a variety of information about the current activity in the application.

Scroll through the window

If a document is too wide or too long to fit within the window, scroll bars will be present along the bottom and/or right of the frame. These can be used to move the hidden parts of the document into the working area.

- Click on the arrows at the ends to nudge the contents slowly in the direction of the arrow.
- Click on the bar to the side of or above or below the slider to move in larger jumps.
- Drag the slider. This is the quickest way to scroll through a large document.

tip

If the typing, drawing or other movements that you make while working on your document take the current position out of the visible area, the document will be scrolled automatically to bring the current position back into view.

Minimize, Maximize and Restore

A window can be in one of three modes.

Switch between them with the buttons at the top right:

Maximize – An application window fills the screen and loses its outer frame. When a document window is maximized, its Title bar is merged with the application Title bar.

Restore – The window is smaller than the full screen or working area. Its size can be adjusted, and it can be moved to any position – within or beyond the limits of the screen.

Minimize – A minimized application becomes a button on the Taskbar. A minimized document shows only the Title bar and window control buttons.

Controlling windows with keys

The Control menu allows you to change the window mode with keystrokes.

1 Press **Alt** and **Space bar** to open the menu in applications.
2 Press **Alt** and the **Minus** key to open the menu for a document.
3 Press the keys of the underlined letters to **Minimize**, **Maximize/Restore** or **Close**. (Or press **Alt + F4** to close.)

- You can also start to **Move** (page 56) or change the **Size** (page 54) of the window from here.

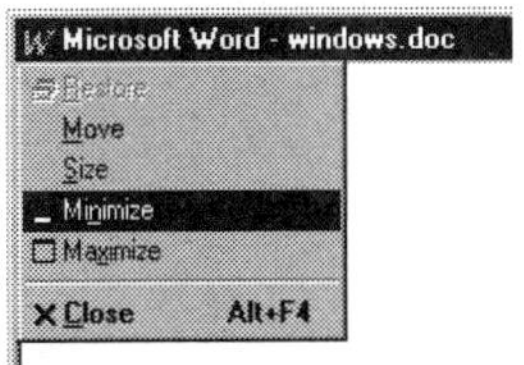

tip

The Control menu can be opened by clicking the icon at the far left of the Title bar, but if you are using the mouse it makes more sense to click the control buttons on the right.

Switch between windows

You can have any number of windows – each running its own program – open at once. You can only ever work on one application at a time – though you can copy or move data between two windows and there may be continuing activities, such as printing, going on in other windows. If you do not need to see what is happening in the other windows, the simplest layout is to run all applications in Maximized mode. The one that you are working on will fill the screen, obscuring the others.

To bring a window to the front:

- Click its button on the Taskbar.

Or

1. Hold down the **Windows** key and press **Tab**. This will select the first Taskbar button – press **Tab** again to move to the next.
2. When the one you want is selected, press **Enter** to open its window.

View multiple windows

If you want to see two or more windows at the same time – perhaps to copy material from one to another – the simplest way is to use the **Cascade** or **Tile** commands. They take the windows currently open in Maximized or Restore mode and arrange them overlapping (**Cascade**), side-by-side (**Tile Horizontally**) or one above the other (**Tile Vertically**).

1 Right-click on a blank area of the Taskbar.

2 Select **Cascade** or **Tile Horizontally/Vertically**.

To return to the previous layout:

3 Right-click the Taskbar again. The menu will now have an **Undo Cascade** or **Undo Tile** command.

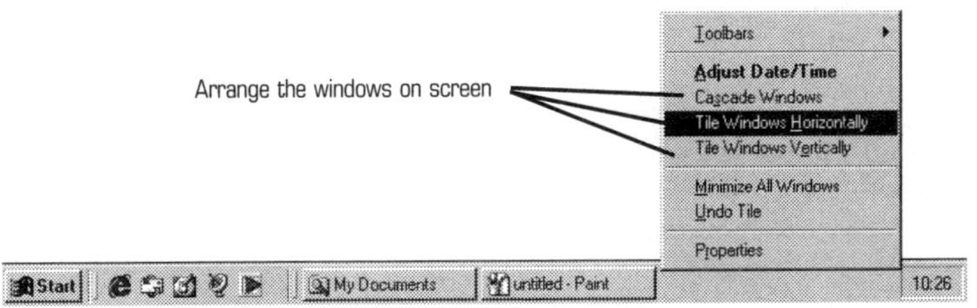

Resize a window with the mouse

When a window is in Restore mode, its size can be adjusted.

1 Point to an edge or corner of the frame – when you are in a suitable place the cursor changes to a double-headed arrow.

2 Hold down the left button and drag the edge or corner to change the window size.

3 Release the mouse button.

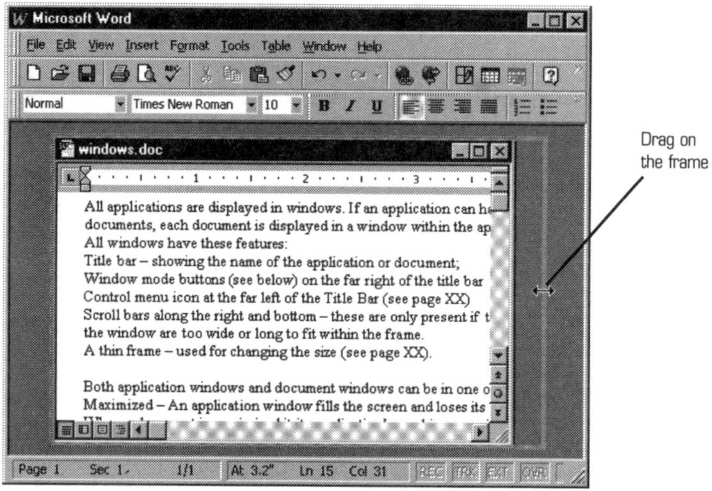

Drag on the frame

Resize with the keyboard

1 Open the Control menu (see page 51).

2 Press **S** to select Size.

3 Press the arrow key corresponding to the edge that you want to move. A double-headed arrow will appear on that edge.

4 Use the arrow keys to move the edge into its new position.

5 Press **Enter** to fix the new size.

tip

If you have turned on the **Show windows contents while dragging** option (on the **Effects** tab of the **Display Properties**, see page 108), the window will change size as you drag or press the arrow keys. If the option is off, you will see a shaded outline showing the new window size.

Move a window

A window in Restore mode can be moved to anywhere on – or part-ways off – the screen (or the working area in an application).

Moving with the mouse

- Point to anywhere on the Title bar and drag the window into its new place.

Moving with the keyboard

1 Open the Control menu and select **Move**.

2 Use the arrow keys to move the window as required.

3 Press **Enter** to fix the new position.

Close a window

When you have finished with a window, close it. This will free up memory so that other applications run more smoothly, as well as reducing the clutter on your Desktop.

There are three methods which will work with any window:

- Click the **Close** button [X] in the top right corner.
- Hold down the **Alt** key and press **F4**.
- Exit from the application – usually with **Exit** or **Close** on the **File** menu.

Managing files

Files and folders

A typical hard drive has 10 Gigabytes of storage, and this must be organized if you are ever to find anything. The organization comes through *folders*. A folder is an elastic-sided division of the disk. It can contain any number of files and subfolders – which can contain other subfolders. At the simplest, a C: drive might contain three folders – *My Documents*, *Program Files* and *Windows* – with each of these having subfolders for different sets of files or programs. You can create new folders, rename, delete or move them to produce your own folder structure.

Understand filenames

Every document's filename has two parts.

The first part of the name can be more or less anything you want and as long as you like (up to 250 characters!). It can consist of any combination of letters, numbers, spaces and underlines, but no other symbols. The name should be meaningful, so that you can easily identify the file when you come back to it later.

The second part is a three-letter extension which identifies the type of document. This is normally set by the application in which it was created, and it is through this extension that Windows can link documents and applications (see page 68).

Some common extensions:

.TXT	Simple text, e.g. from NotePad
.DOC	Word document
.HTM	Web page
.BMP	bitmap image, e.g. from Paint
.GIF	a standard format for image on Web pages
.JPG	an alternative format for Web page images
.WAV	audio file in Wave format
.EXE	an executable program – not a document!

Open My Computer

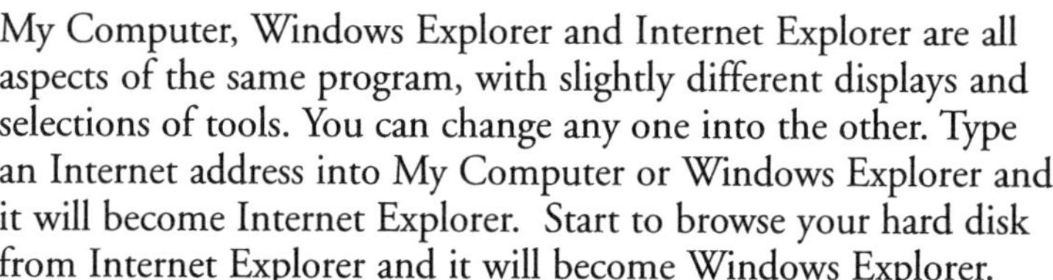

My Computer, Windows Explorer and Internet Explorer are all aspects of the same program, with slightly different displays and selections of tools. You can change any one into the other. Type an Internet address into My Computer or Windows Explorer and it will become Internet Explorer. Start to browse your hard disk from Internet Explorer and it will become Windows Explorer.

My Computer can only be started from the Desktop icon. It is Windows Explorer at its simplest, with the display set to just show the contents of one drive or folder.

My Computer

If you set My Computer so that it opens a new window for every folder (one of the *Folder Options*, see page 64), it can also be used for reorganizing your file storage.

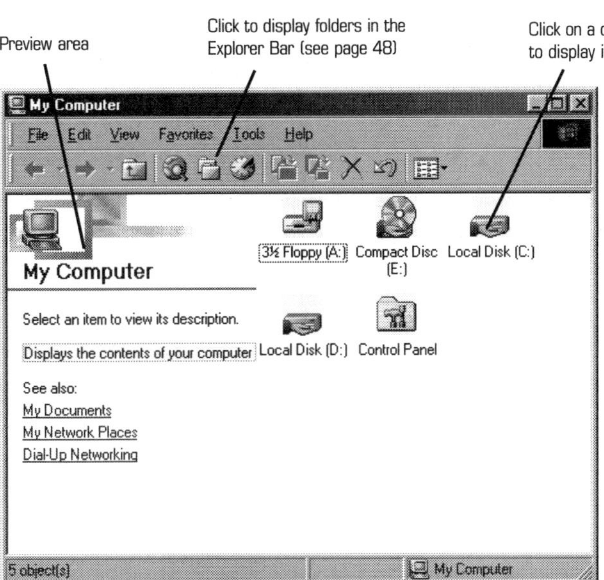

MY COMPUTER IN WEB PAGE VIEW, WITH LARGE ICONS, AND THE ADDRESS TOOLBAR AND THE EXPLORER BAR TURNED OFF

Explore your folders

You can manage your files and folders much better if you display the *Folders* in the Explorer Bar (which turns My Computer into Windows Explorer).

1 Click [Folders] to display Folders in the Explorer Bar.

2 In the folder display, [+] to the left of a folder name shows that it has subfolders. Click this to open up the branch. The icon changes to [–] – click this to close the branch.

When a folder is selected, its files and subfolders are listed in the main pane. Files can be listed by name, type, date or size, and displayed as thumbnails or large or small icons, with or without details (see page 66).

The **Status bar** at the bottom shows the number of objects in the folder and the amount of memory they use, or the size of a selected file.

If you run Windows Explorer (on the Accessories menu), it opens with the Explorer Bar turned on.

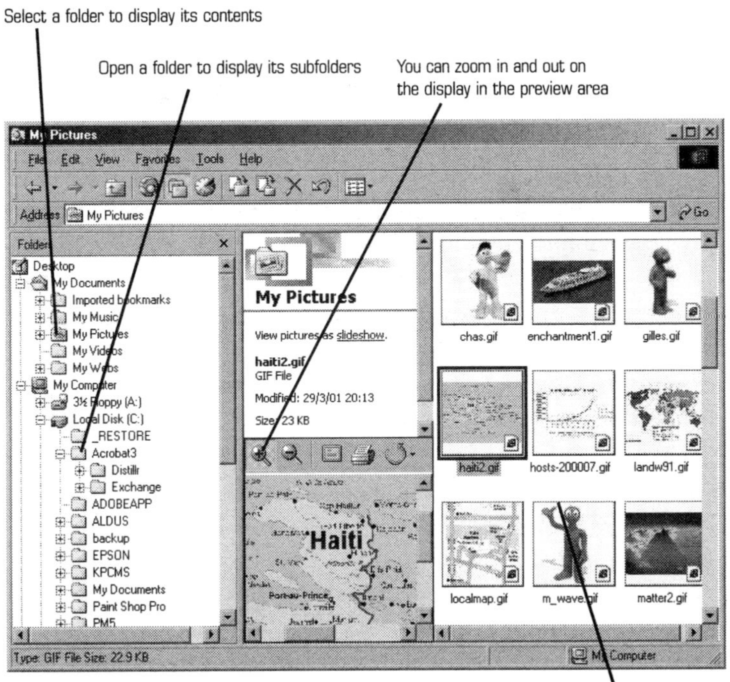

WITH THE EXPLORER BAR TURNED ON, MY COMPUTER BECOMES WINDOWS EXPLORER

Set your Folder Options

This panel lets you control the behaviour and appearance of My Computer/Windows Explorer (and of the Desktop).

- To reach it, open the **Tools** menu and select **Folder Options**.

In the **Click items...** section, set how you want the computer to respond to single and double-clicks. I would recommend:

- **Open with a single click** if you are a new user – it's simpler.
- **Double-click to open** if you have previously used earlier versions of Windows – it's the familiar way of working.

In the **Web View** section, **Enable Web content in folders** for a 'richer' experience, with decorated folders and previews of files. Use **Windows classic folders** for a simpler file display.

The **Browse Folders** option only applies when the Explorer Bar is turned off. **Open each folder in its own window** is useful for moving files from one to another, but can produce a cluttered screen. If you select **Open each folder in the same window**, you can make it open in a new window if you hold down **Control** when opening the folder.

- When you have set the options, click **OK** to close the panel.

Select **Enable Web content on my desktop** if you want to use an HTML page as a background (see page 102)

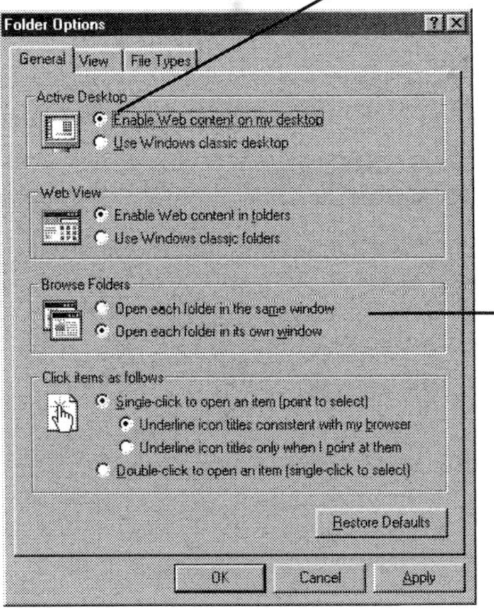

Whichever option you set, you can make My Computer do the other by holding down Control when you open the folder

THE FOLDER OPTIONS SET FOR A WEB-STYLE DISPLAY

Set your folder views

Click **Like Current Folder** if you want its View and other settings to be applied to all folders.

Click **Reset All Folders** to go back to the original settings.

Advanced Settings

Most of these should be left at their defaults but note these:

Hidden files – Windows Me 'hides' essential files and (crucial) system, to prevent accidental deletion. They can be shown if you do want to see them.

Remember each folder's view settings will retain the separate options from one session to the next. The settings can be different for each folder, for example you may want more detail in folders that contain documents than in those that contain program files.

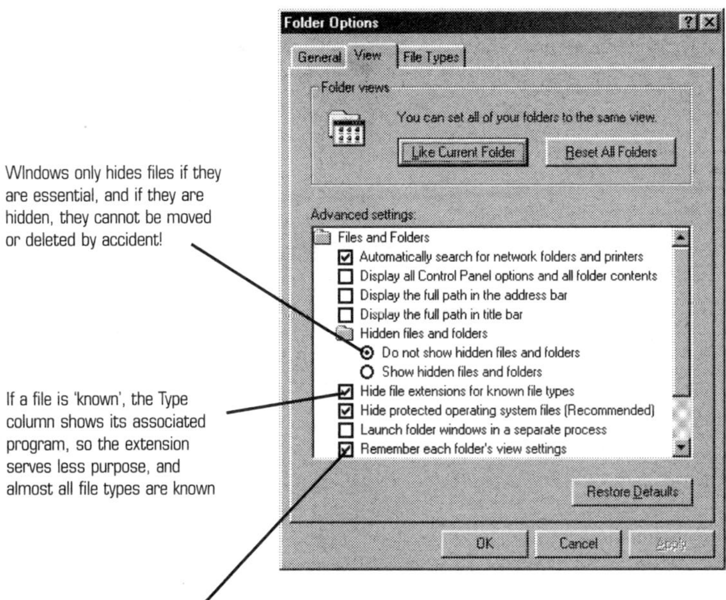

Turn this on if you want to use different views in different folders

Understand file types

Documents can be associated with applications, so that picking one from the **Documents** list on the **Start** menu or from a folder will start up its application and open the document within it.

The **File Types** tab lists all the 'registered' file types – the ones associated with applications. Select one from the list, and in the bottom of the panel you will see the application that the document **Opens with**.

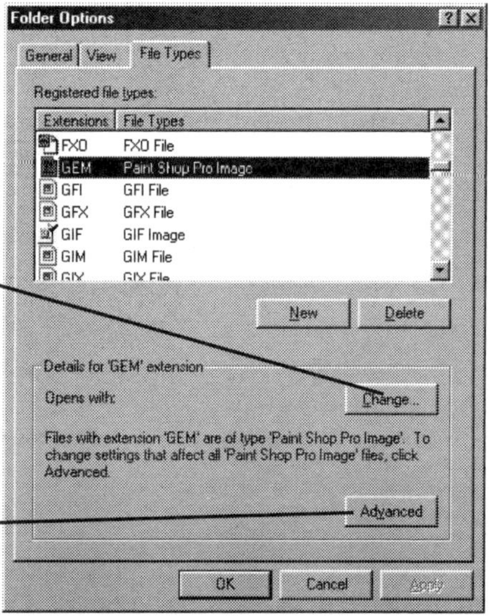

To change the settings for the selected extension, click Change and give the new details at the dialog box

Several extensions may be associated with one application – use the **Advanced** button to change the settings for them all

Associate file types

If a program's installation routine doesn't set up the association for you, you can do it yourself. This is possible through the **New** button on the **File Types** tab, but there is an easier way. Close the **Folder Options** panel for now.

1 Later, when you try to open a document of an unregistered type, you will be presented with the **Open With** panel.

2 Select an application – if it is not listed, but you know that it is on your PC, click the **Other...** button and track down the program file.

4 If you want to give a description (to appear in the **File Types** list), do so.

5 Click **OK**.

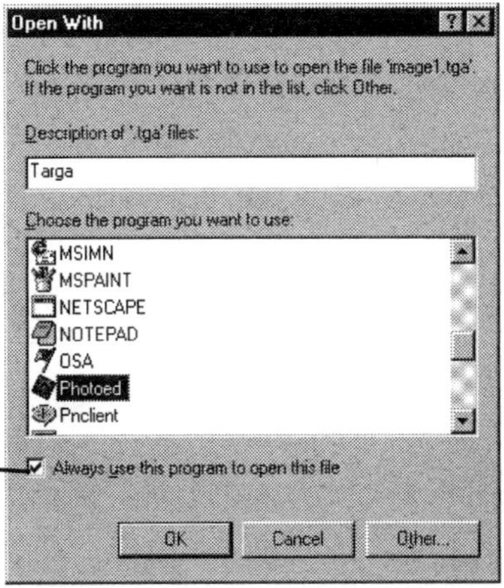

If you do not want to set up a permanent link with an application, clear this box and the document will be opened with the chosen program on this occasion only

The tools

- **Back** and **Forward** move between the last folders that you have opened.
- **Up** takes you up to the next level folder.
- **Move To** moves the selected file to a folder picked from a list at the next stage.
- **Copy To** copies the selected file to another folder.
- **Delete** moves the selected file or folder into the Recycle Bin (page 85).
- **Undo** undoes thc previous action, if possible.
- **Views** drops down a list of the main View options.

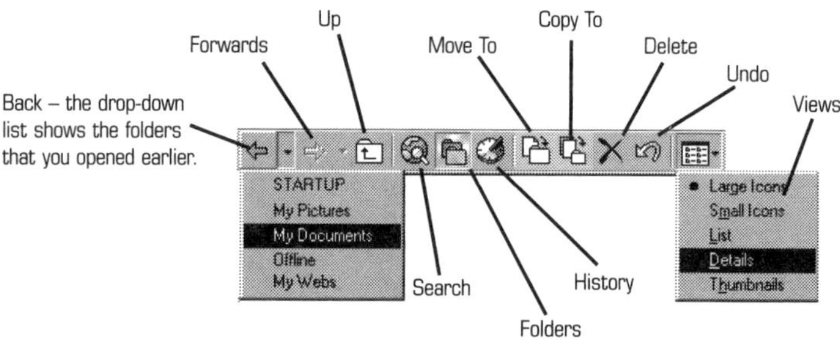

HISTORY (AND, TO A LESSER EXTENT, **SEARCH**) ARE MAINLY USED WHEN EXPLORING THE INTERNET

Set your View options

Files and folders can be shown in various ways:

- *Large icons* (as in the screenshot on page 61) are easier to see and larger targets if you are less than accurate with the mouse!
- *Small icons* and *List* differ only in the order – listing either across or down the screen. Both are good for selecting sets of files.
- *Details* gives a column display under the headings Name, Size, Type and Modified. The files can be sorted into order of any of these (see page 72).
- *Thumbnails* (as in the screenshot on page 63) shows – if possible – a miniature image of each file. It is, of course, best for use with images, but it can be handy for Web pages and some formatted documents.

Set the style from the **View** menu or the **View** drop-down list.

Sort files into order

In Details View you can sort the files into ascending or descending order by name, size, type or date.

1 Open the **View** menu or the **View** drop-down list and select **Details**.

2 Click on a column heading to sort the files in ascending order by that feature.

3 Click a second time on the same heading to sort them in descending order.

tip

When you want to tidy up an over-filled folder, sort it by age or type to group together sets of files for moving or deleting.

Click on the heading to sort – the arrow shows the direction of the sort order

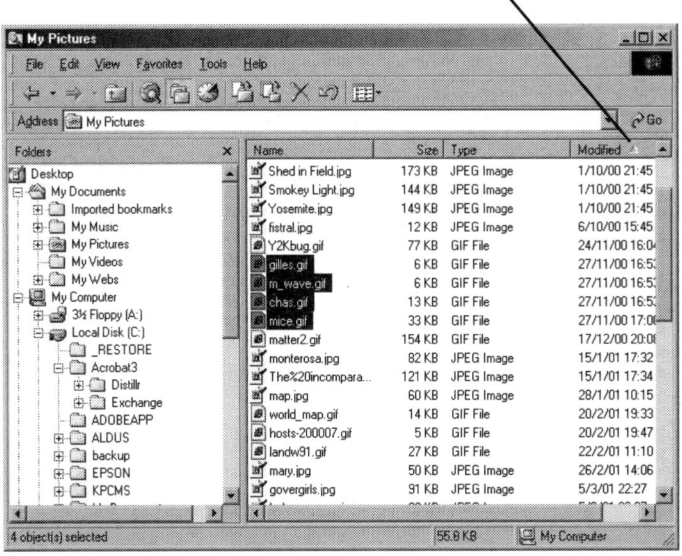

Organize your folders

Windows Me sets up one folder for your files, called *My Documents*. This is unlikely to be enough for very long. You need to create more folders if:

- you will be storing more than a few dozen documents – it's hard to find stuff in crowded folders;
- more than one person uses the PC – everyone should have their own storage space;
- your documents fall into distinct categories – personal, hobbies, different areas of work, etc.

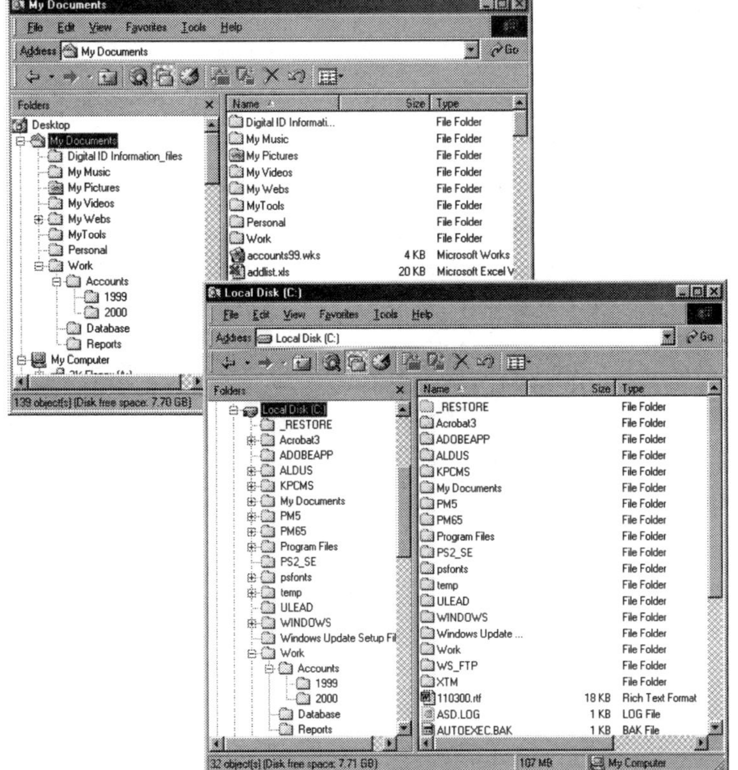

TWO APPROACHES TO A FOLDER STRUCTURE: IN THE TOP ONE, THE NEW FOLDERS HAVE BEEN CREATED WITHIN *MY DOCUMENTS*; IN THE LOWER, THE FOLDERS ARE ALL AT THE MAIN LEVEL. EITHER WORKS JUST AS WELL

Create a folder

A new folder can be created at any point in the folder structure.

1 In the Folder list in the Explorer Bar, select the folder which will contain the new one.

2 Open the **File** menu, point to **New** then select **Folder.**

3 Replace *New Folder* with a meaningful name.

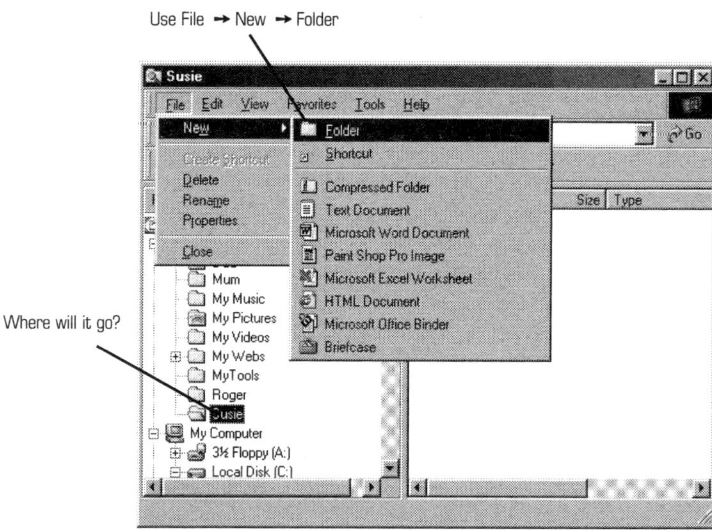

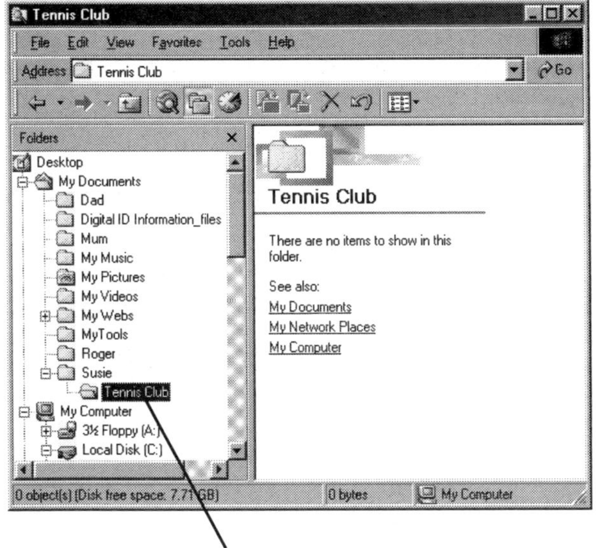

Give it a meaningful name

tip

If you decide the folder is in the wrong place, select it and drag it into place in the Folders list.

Move files to another folder

Have the Explorer Bar open, displaying the folder list.

1 Select the file(s).
2 Scroll through the Folder display and/or open subfolders, if necessary, until you can see the target folder.
3 Drag the file(s) across the screen until the target folder is highlighted, then drop it there.

tip

If you don't know how to select several files at once, see *Select graphics or icons*, page 28.

tip

Files are only copied if the target is on the same disk. If it is on another disk, the files are moved (see page 81).

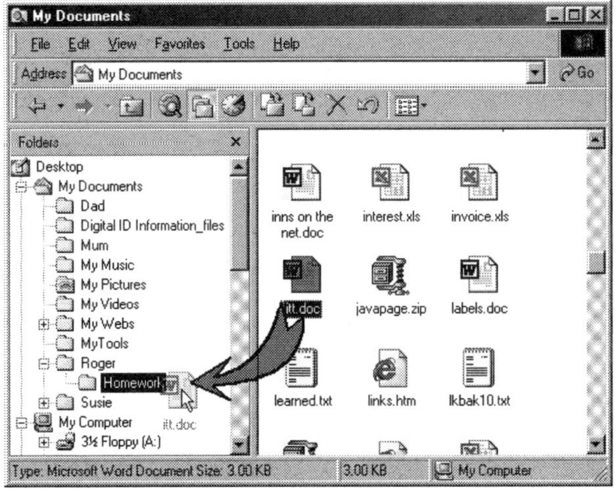

IF YOU CAN SEE THE TARGET FOLDER, YOU CAN DRAG FILES INTO IT

Copy files to a floppy

Have the Explorer Bar open, displaying the folder list.

1 Place a formatted disk (see page 185) in the A: drive.

2 Select the file(s).

3 Scroll through the Folder display until you can see the A: drive.

3 Drag the file(s) across the screen until the A: drive icon is highlighted, then drop it there.

Copy files on the same disk

Have the Explorer Bar open, displaying the folder list.

1 Select the file(s).

2 Set the Folder display so that you can see the target folder.

3 Hold down the right mouse button and drag the file(s) onto the target folder.

4 Release the button. A shortcut menu appears.

5 Select **Copy Here.**

- The file will be named *Copy of…* followed by its orignal name. Edit this if required.

tip

To ***move*** a file from one disk to another, hold down the right mouse button while you drag. When you drop the file, select **Move Here** from the short menu.

Copy To or Move To Folder

A slower, but more reliable alternative to drag and drop is to use the **Copy To** and **Move To Folder** commands.

1 Select the file(s).

2 To move a file, click , or open the **Edit** menu and select **Move to Folder…**

3 To copy, click or open the **Edit** menu and select **Copy to Folder…**

4 The **Browse For Folder** dialog box will open. Work your way down through the folder structure and select the target folder, then click **OK**.

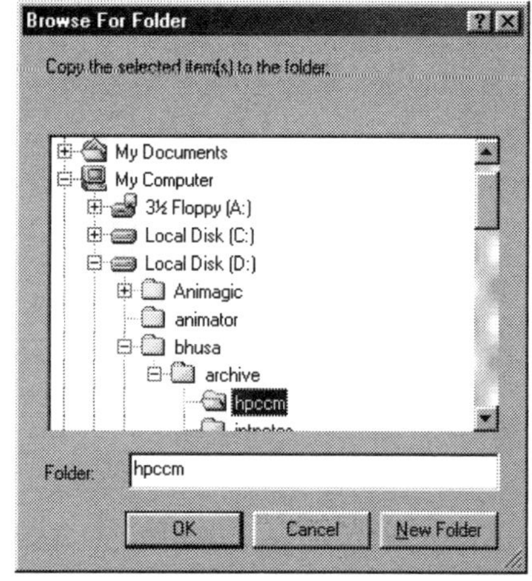

Rename a file

1 Select the file and press the **F2** key.

or

2 Right-click on the file and select **Rename**.

3 Change the name and press **Enter**.

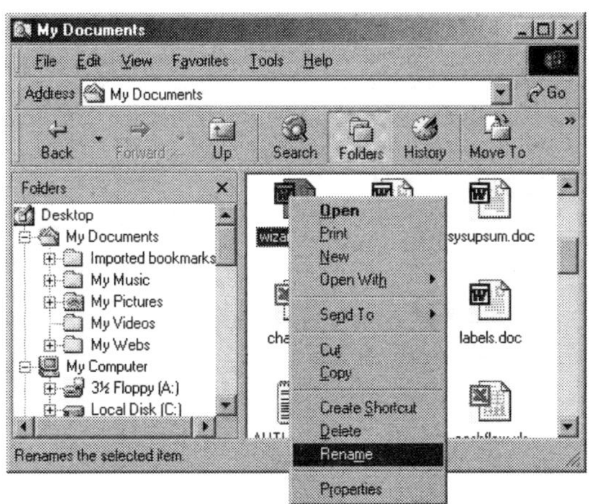

tip

When renaming files, do not change their extensions! If you do, you will lose the document–application link (page 68).

Send files elsewhere

The **Send To** command on the **File** menu (or on the shortcut menu) offers a simple way to copy a file to a floppy disk, to send one by e-mail, or to start uploading a page to your Web space.

Just select the destination to begin! Once you've started the file on its way, the rest of the process runs through as normal.

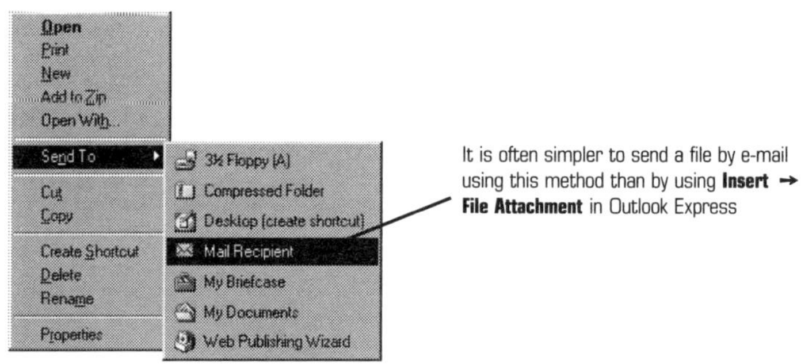

It is often simpler to send a file by e-mail using this method than by using **Insert → File Attachment** in Outlook Express

Delete files

If a file is no longer needed, select it and press the **Delete** or **Backspace** key or use the **Delete** command on the **File** menu.

Windows Me makes it very difficult to delete files by accident!

- You have to confirm – or cancel – the deletion at the prompt.
- And nothing is actually deleted at this stage. Instead, the file or folder is moved to the Recycle Bin. Let's look at that now.

tip

If you delete a folder, all its files are also deleted.

Use the Recycle Bin

The Recycle Bin allows you to recover files deleted in error. You'll rarely need it, but when you do, you will be glad that it is there!

To restore a deleted file:

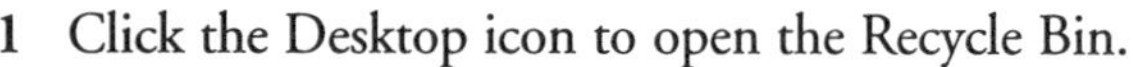

1 Click the Desktop icon to open the Recycle Bin.

2 Select the file.

3 Open the **File** menu, or right-click for the shortcut menu and select **Restore**.

- If the file's folder has also been deleted, it will be re-created first, so that the file can go back where it came from.

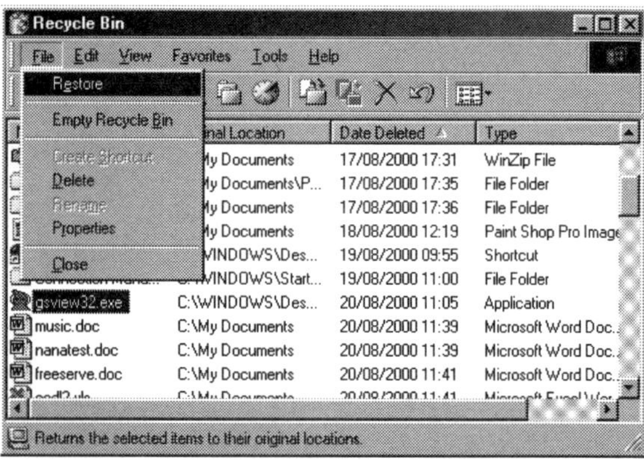

Empty the Bin

One of the main reasons for deleting files is to free up disk space, but as long as they are in the Recycle Bin, they are still on the disk. So, make a habit of emptying the bin regularly.

1 Open the Bin and check its contents carefully and restore any accidental deletions.

2 Open the **File** menu and select **Empty Recycle Bin**.

tip

The default settings lets the Recycle Bin use 10% of the drive's capacity. If you want to change this, right-click on the Bin's icon to open its Properties panel and set the level there.

Search for a file

The **Search for File or Folders** routine can track down lost files for you, hunting for them by name, location, contents, date, type and/or size.

1 In Explorer, click the Search icon.

Or

2 Click **Start**, point to **Search** and select **For Files or Folders…**

3 Enter all or part of the filename or some text from within the file – or a combination of the two.

- For example, if you were looking for a letter to 'Mr Ree', you would know that it contained his name and that it was a Word document. You could simply give 'Mr Ree' as the Containing text, but if you type 'doc' in the filename slot, it will speed things up, as the search would then only have to read through document files.

4 If you specify the drives or folders to start looking in, it will speed up the search. And note that the search will normally look into all the subfolders below the start point.

5 Click **Search Now** to start the search.

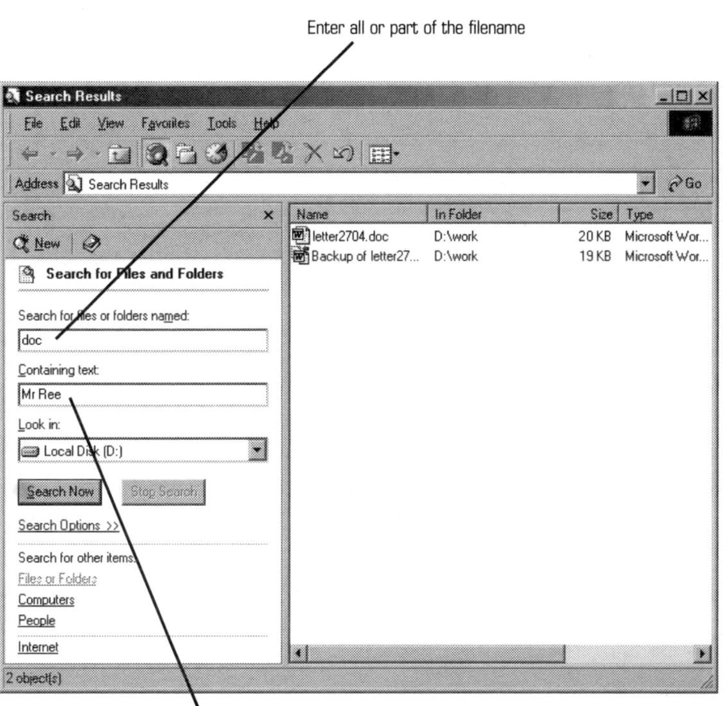

If there are any names or special words in the text that will identify the file, enter them here

Search for files by date

Specify the date if you know when you created or last worked on the file and you want to speed up the search.

1 Click **Search Options>>** to open the options panel.

2 Tick **Date** to open its settings area.

3 In the drop-down list, set to search for when the file was **Modified**, **Created** or **Last Accessed**.

4 Set a **month** or **days** limit.

Or

5 Set the dates **between** which to search.

6 Click **Search Now**.

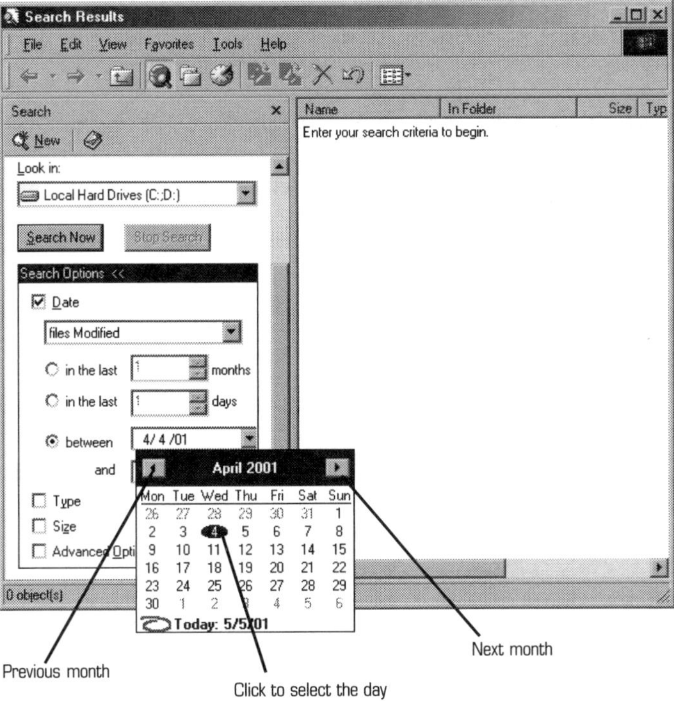

DATES ARE SELECTED FROM THE CALENDAR DISPLAYS

Search for files by type or size

1 Click **<u>Search Options>></u>** to open the options panel.
2 Tick **Type** to open its settings area.
3 In the drop-down list, select to type of file.
4 Tick **Size** to see its options.
5 Set the **at least** or **at most** limit.
6 Click **Search Now**.

tip

You search purely by type or size, but these options are normally used to restrict a search that otherwise might turn up too many results.

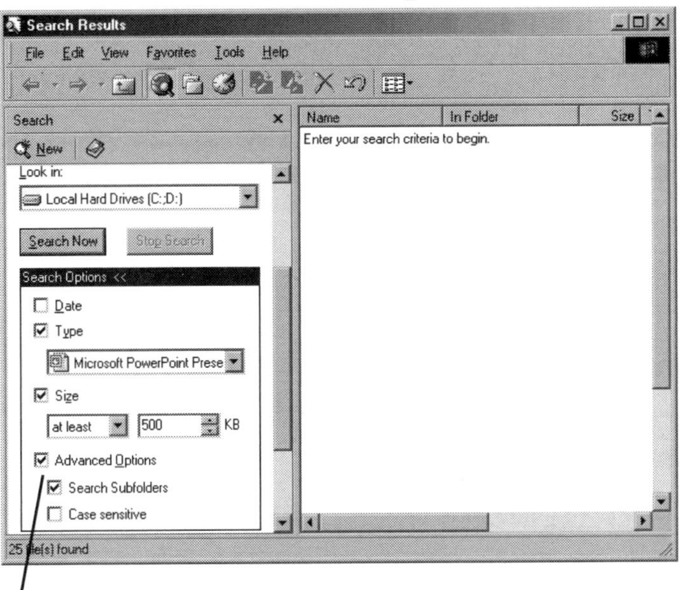

The **Advanced Options** are best left at their defaults:

If you turn off **Search Subfolders**, it will only search the top level of a disk;

if you turn on **Case sensitive**, filenames must be written in the same combinations of lower-case and capital letters to match

Create shortcuts

A Desktop shortcut offers the simplest and quickest way to start an application or open a folder – as long as you can see the Desktop! You can create new shortcuts in several ways. This is probably the easiest.

Application shortcuts

1 Open the application's folder in Explorer or My Computer.
2 Locate the program file. If you are not sure whether it is thc right one, click (or double-click) on it. If the application runs, it's the right file.
3 Drag the file onto the Desktop.
4 Edit the name to remove '*Shortcut to...*'.

Shortcuts to folders

1 Select the folder in Explorer or My Computer.
2 Hold the right mouse button down and drag the icon onto the Desktop.
3 Select **Create Shortcut(s) Here**.

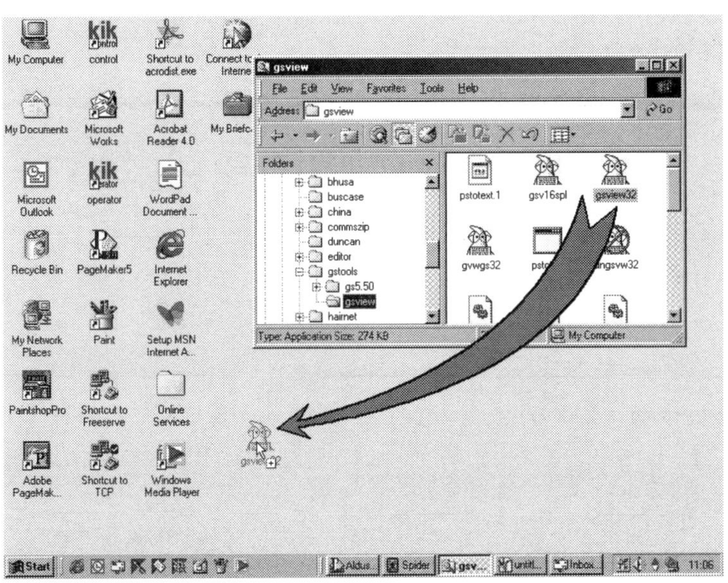

CREATING A DESKTOP SHORTCUT USING WINDOWS EXPLORER

CUSTOMIZING

The Control Panel

Open the panel

Click the **Start** button, point to **Settings** and select **Control Panel**.

If your folders are in Web mode, only most commonly used components are visible at first – click **view all Control Panel options** to see the rest.

Click the links or the icons to open their **Properties** panels where you can view and edit the settings.

The Control Panel remains open until you close it with **File → Close** or by clicking [X].

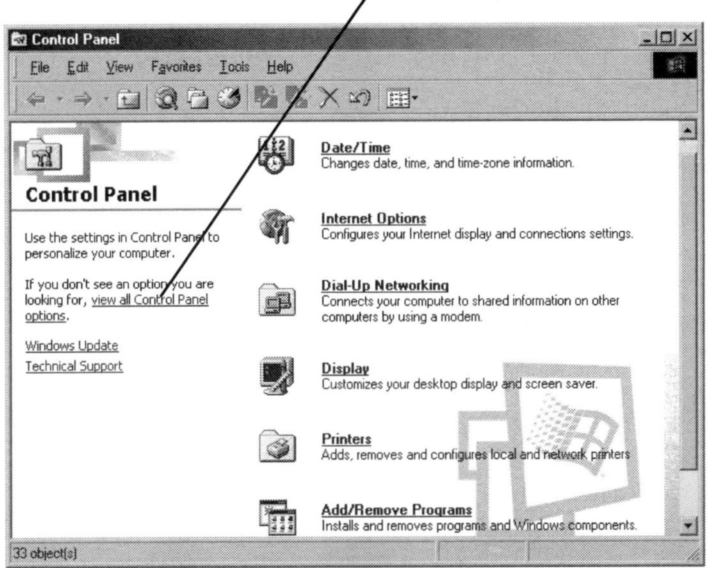

THE CONTROL PANEL, WHEN FIRST OPENED IN WEB MODE, AND SHOWING ONLY THE MORE COMMONLY ADJUSTED OPTIONS. FOR INTERNET OPTIONS AND DIAL-UP NETWORKING, SEE THE COMPANION BOOK, *QUICK FIX: INTERNET EXPLORER 5.5/OUTLOOK EXPRESS 5*

Set the date and time

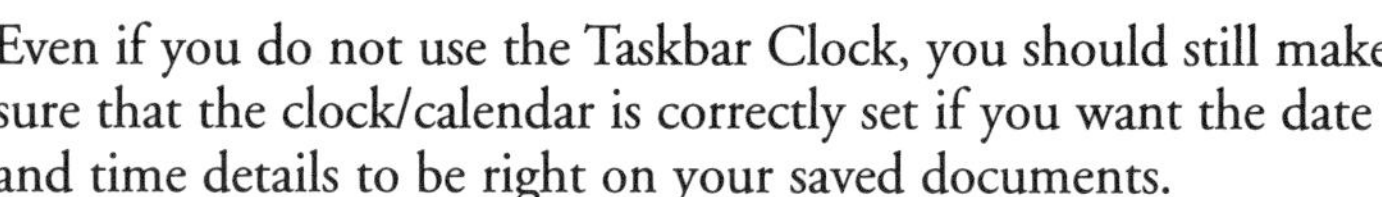

Even if you do not use the Taskbar Clock, you should still make sure that the clock/calendar is correctly set if you want the date and time details to be right on your saved documents.

PCs are good time-keepers – Windows Me even adjusts for Summer Time automatically – as long as they are set correctly at the start. Open the **Date/Time** Properties panel and check yours.

- To change the date, select the month from the drop-down list, and click on the day.
- To change the time, select the hour digits and use the arrow buttons, then repeat with the minute and seconds digits.
- To change the Time Zone, select a different one from the drop-down list.

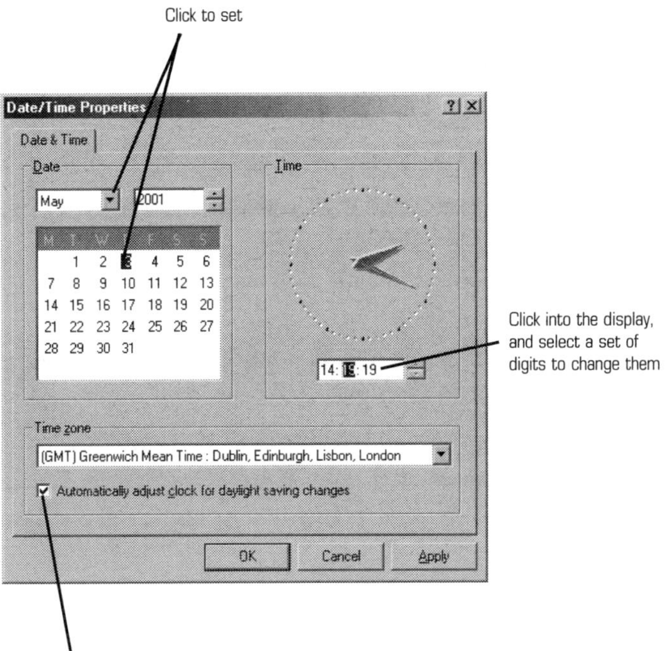
Click to set
Date/Time Properties
Date & Time
Date
May
2001
M T W T F S S
1 2 3 4 5 6
7 8 9 10 11 12 13
14 15 16 17 18 19 20
21 22 23 24 25 26 27
28 29 30 31
Time
14:19:19
Click into the display, and select a set of digits to change them
Time zone
(GMT) Greenwich Mean Time : Dublin, Edinburgh, Lisbon, London
Automatically adjust clock for daylight saving changes
OK
Cancel
Apply
Turn this on and let Windows change the clock for you when Summer Time starts and ends

Adjust the Display – the Background

The background is purely decorative. It can be a plain colour, a single picture, a small image 'tiled' to fill the screen or an HTML document. Windows has some suitable images and HTML pages, but any JPG, GIF or BMP image or Web page can be used.

1 Click the Display icon to open the **Display Properties** panel. The **Background** tab should be on top.

2 Scroll through the list of images and pages. If one sounds interesting, select it to see its preview.

- With a small image, set the **Display** mode to **Tile**. The image will be repeated across and down to fill the screen.
- With a larger image, set the **Display** mode to **Center** to see it in its natural size, or **Stretch** to make it fill the screen.

3 Click **Apply** to test the choice. If you don't like it, try another.

Don't click **OK** until you have worked through all the tabs. Clicking **OK** will close the Display Properties panel.

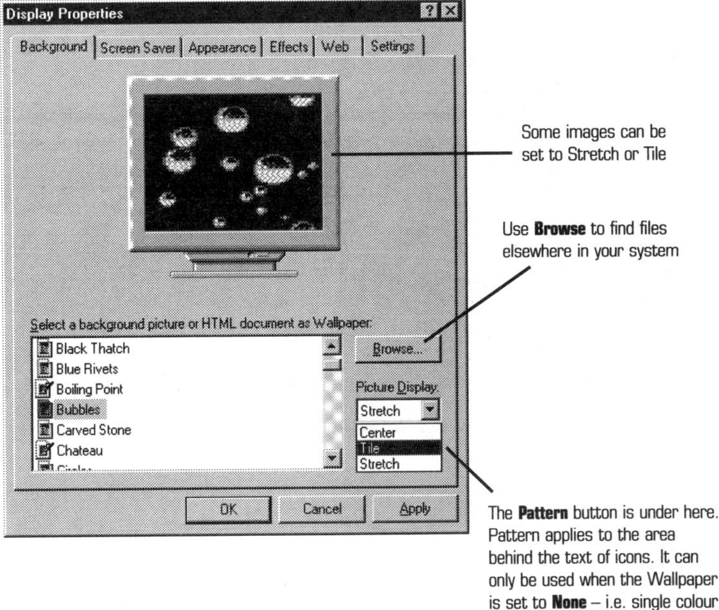

Some images can be set to Stretch or Tile

Use **Browse** to find files elsewhere in your system

The **Pattern** button is under here. Pattern applies to the area behind the text of icons. It can only be used when the Wallpaper is set to **None** – i.e. single colour background

THE BACKGROUND TAB, WITH THE DISPLAY OPTIONS VISIBLE

Change the Screen Saver

A screen saver is a moving image that takes over the screen if the computer is left unattended for a while. On older monitors this prevented a static image from burning a permanent ghost image into the screen. Newer monitors do not suffer from this – in fact, most will turn themselves off if the computer is left idle.

The Screen Saver can be password protected, so that it will lock the screen – and the rest of the system – until the password is entered. This can be useful if you do not want passers-by to read your screen while you are away from your desk.

1 Switch to the **Screen Saver** tab.

2 Select a saver from the drop-down list.

3 Click **Preview** for a full screen demo.

4 Click **Settings...** to set the timing, colour or other options.

5 Set the time to **Wait** before activating the saver.

6 Tick **Password Protected**, then click **Change** to set a password, if required.

7 Click **Apply**.

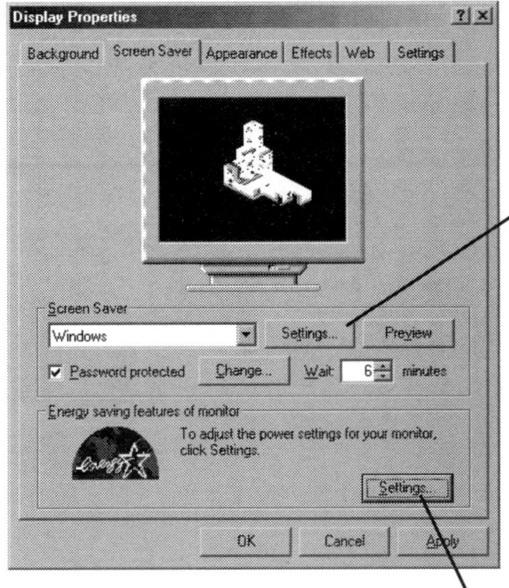

The **Settings** have options for the speed, colour, text or other features, depending on the choice of Screen Saver

If your monitor has Energy saving, use this **Settings** button to set when the screen should turn itself off. You may also be able to turn the hard disk off to save power. Both screen and hard disk will wake up and be ready, exactly as you left them, when you want to start work again

Set the Appearance

Use this panel to set the colour and fonts for the Desktop and standard elements in all applications – menus, dialog boxes, etc. There are a couple of dozen ready-made schemes, including high contrast schemes, some with large fonts, for greater visibility.

1 Switch to the **Appearance** tab.

2 Select a **Scheme** from the drop-down list.

3 To redefine an individual **Item**, select it from the drop-down list then set its **Size**, **Color** or **Font**.

4 Click **Apply**.

tip

If it takes you a while to get everything 'just so', click the **Save As...** button and save the settings as a scheme. If someone later changes the settings, you can restore the appearance by selecting your saved scheme.

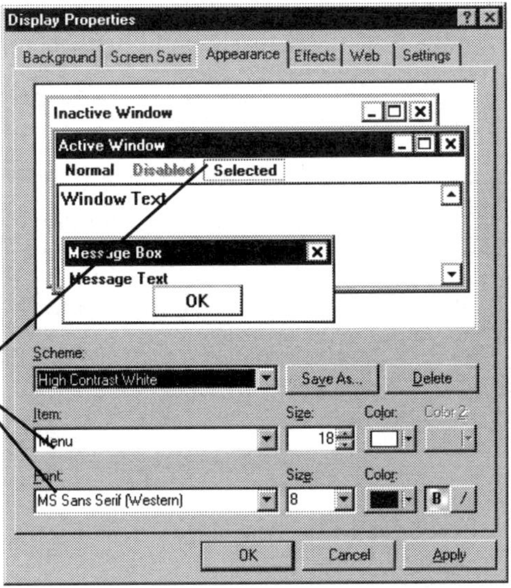

Select an item by clicking on the screen or picking from the **Item** list, if you want to change its font, size or colour

Adjust the Effects

Here you can change the images used for the Desktop icons, if you like.

1 Switch to the **Effects** tab.

2 Select a **Desktop icon** from the display.

3 Click **Change Icon…**

4 Pick a new image, if you can find a better one, and click **OK**.

5 In the Visual Effects section, turn on **Use large icons** if you need the extra visibility.

6 Click **Apply**.

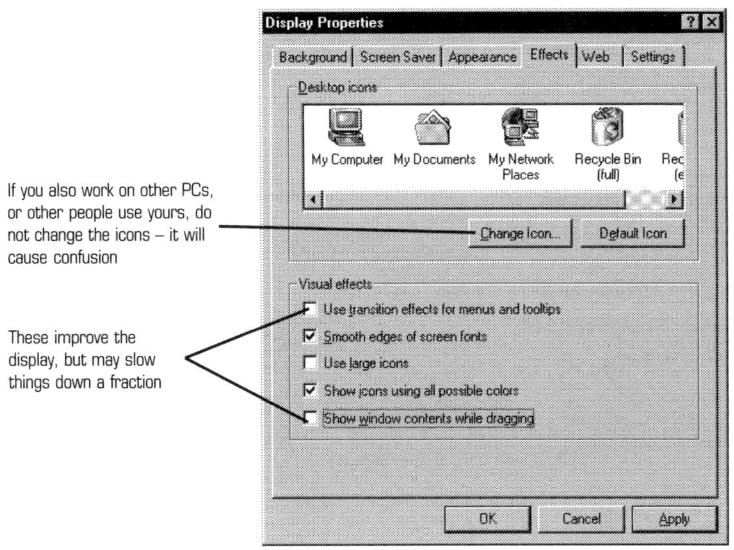
If you also work on other PCs, or other people use yours, do not change the icons – it will cause confusion
These improve the display, but may slow things down a fraction
Display Properties
Background
Screen Saver
Appearance
Effects
Web
Settings
Desktop icons
My Computer
My Documents
My Network Places
Recycle Bin (full)
Change Icon...
Default Icon
Visual effects
Use transition effects for menus and tooltips
Smooth edges of screen fonts
Use large icons
Show icons using all possible colors
Show window contents while dragging
OK
Cancel
Apply

Set the Web options

If you turn on **Show Web content on my Active Desktop** you can then select the Active Desktop elements to include. At first, there will only be one listed – *My Current Home Page*.

The Active Desktop concept has not been hugely popluar, but there are some components available from Microsoft and a few other sites. To see what they are like, go online and click the **New** button. This will link you to Microsoft's Active Desktop area, where you will find components to download.

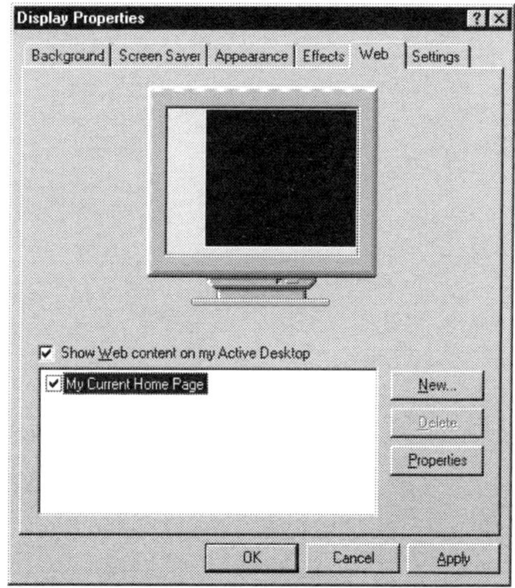

The icon names are underlined, showing that they respond to a single click

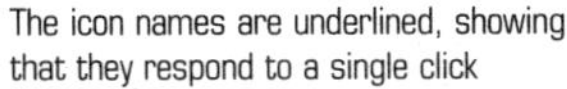

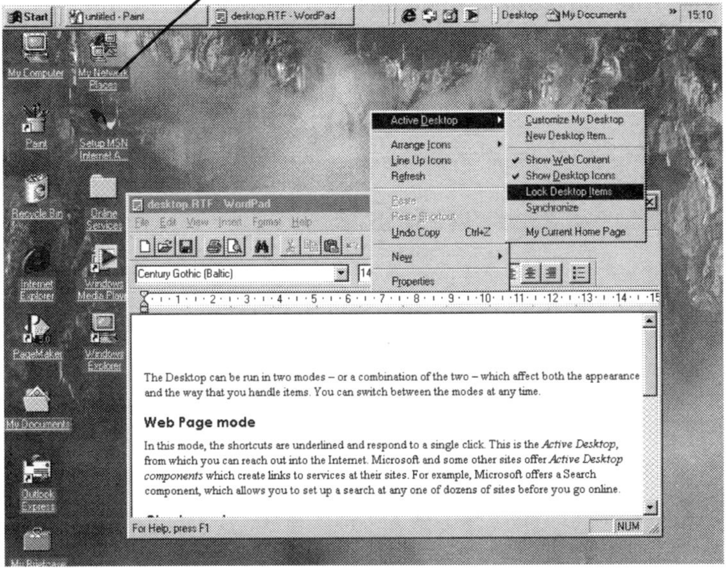

HERE, THE DESKTOP HAS BEEN GIVEN A NEW BACKGROUND AND THE TASKBAR HAS BEEN MOVED TO THE TOP OF THE SCREEN WITH THE DESKTOP TOOLBAR ADDED TO IT. THIS DUPLICATES THE ICONS ON THE DESKTOP – WHICH MEANS YOU CAN STILL REACH THEM WHEN AN APPLICATION FILLS THE SCREEN. (SEE PAGES 135 TO 141 FOR MORE ON THE TASKBAR.)

Adjust the Settings

The Settings relate to the size of the screen and number of colours used in the display. They should normally be left alone as Windows Me will select the optimum settings for your system – and the **Advanced** settings should certainly be left at their defaults unless you know and understand the details of your system. Bad selections here can really mess up your screen!

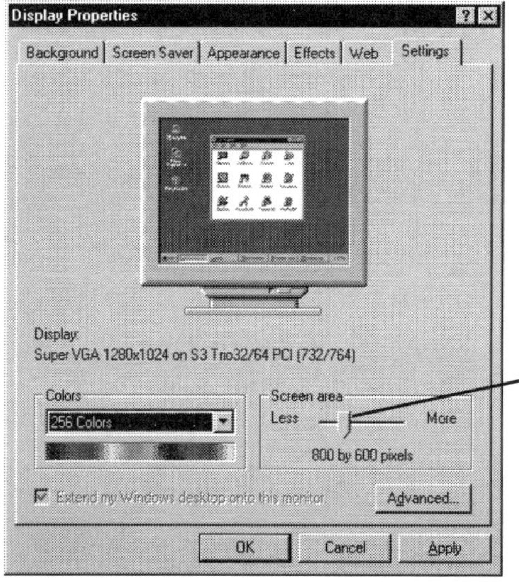

The Screen area is set low as this works better for the small pictures I need for this book. 1024 by 768 or 1280 by 1024 work better on a 17" monitor

Improve Accessibility

The Accessibility options can make life easier for anyone who is less than comfortable with the keyboard or mouse.

Keyboard

StickyKeys will 'hold down' the **Shift**, **Ctrl** or **Alt** keys while you press the next to get a keyboard shortcut combination.

FilterKeys control the point at which keystrokes are picked up, or are repeated, and the repeat rate. (See also *Adjust the keyboard*, page 124).

ToggleKeys will make sounds when the **Caps Lock**, **Num Lock** or **Scroll Lock** keys are pressed.

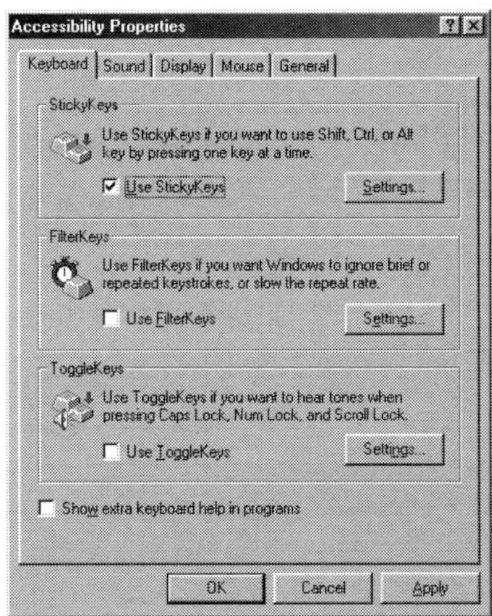

Sound

The main option on this tab turns on visual clues to replace or emphasize sound prompts.

Display

The high contrast display options, which are also available on the Display Properties panel (page 102), can be turned on here.

Mouse

The **MouseKeys** option lets the Number pad keys mimic mouse actions. The central key (5) is the left click; minus and 5 are the right-click; the numbers (7, 8, 9, 4, 6, 1, 2, 3) move the mouse.

General

If you have set up an accessibility option so that it can be toggled on and off as required, go to this tab to define when to turn options off, and how to notify you of their status. If you have a device plugged into your serial port, to use in place of the standard keyboard or mouse, it can be set up through this tab.

Add or remove a program

New programs are best installed through their setup routines. Use the **Add/Remove Programs** panel to *uninstall* software. If you simply delete a program's folder, it may remove all or most of the software's files – some may be elsewhere in your disks – but it will not remove the Start menu entry or the File Types associations.

1 Click **Add/ Remove Programs.**

2 Select the software to be uninstalled.

3 Click **Add/Remove…**

4 Confirm the removal at the prompt.

◆ With some software you can then select which components to uninstall; with others the whole package is simply removed.

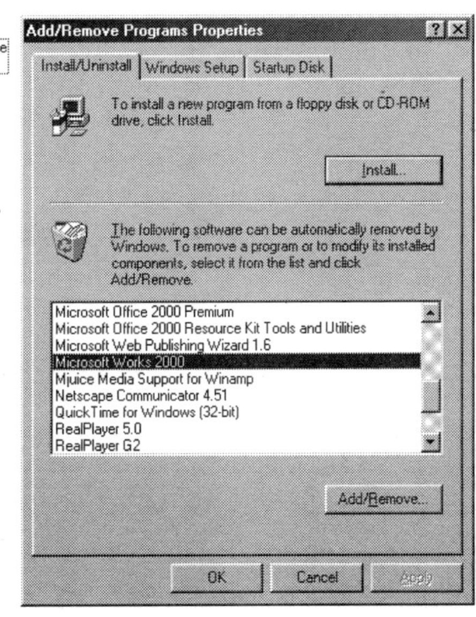

Adjust the Windows Setup

After using Windows Me for a while, you may decide that some components are a waste of space, but that there are others that you need and which have not been installed.

1 Find your Windows CD and go to the **Windows Setup** tab of the **Add/Remove Programs** panel.

2 Select a **Component** and click **Details...**

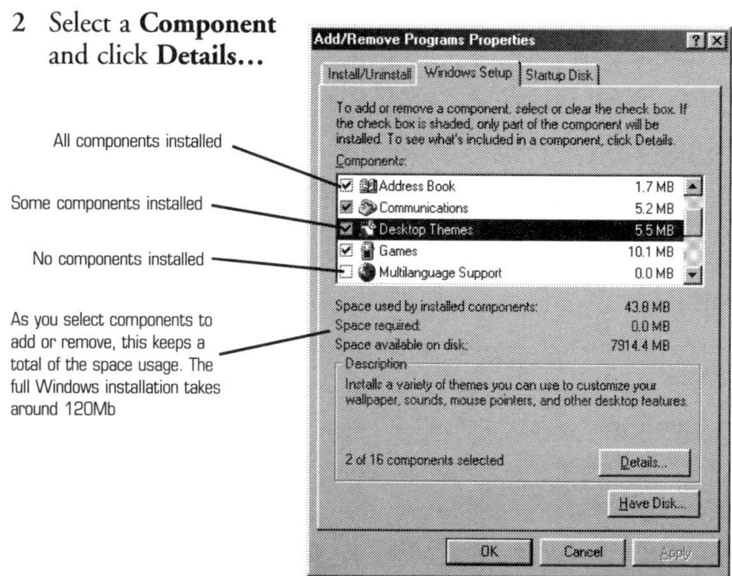

3 At the next panel, tick the checkbox to add a component, or clear it to remove an existing one, then click **OK**.

4 Click **OK** on the main panel when you have done, and wait while Windows adds or removes components. You may have to restart the PC for some changes to take effect.

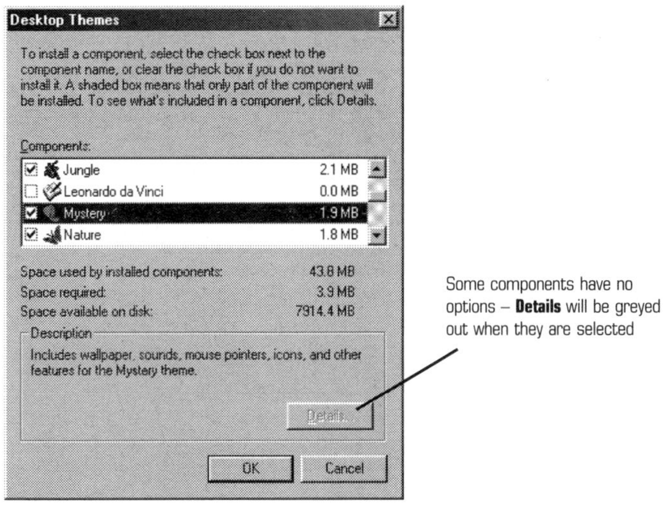

Some components have no options – **Details** will be greyed out when they are selected

Add a Desktop theme

A theme will give a consistent look to your Desktop, its icons and screen saver, as well as mouse pointers, sounds and the fonts used in Windows – though you don't have to apply all aspects of the theme. Themes are installed through the Windows Setup routine. The **Desktop Themes** panel simply lets you change or adjust the theme.

1 Click **Desktop Themes**.

2 Select the theme from the drop-down list at the top.

3 Preview the screen saver, mouse pointers and sounds.

4 Clear the checkboxes for any parts that you do not want.

5 Click **OK**.

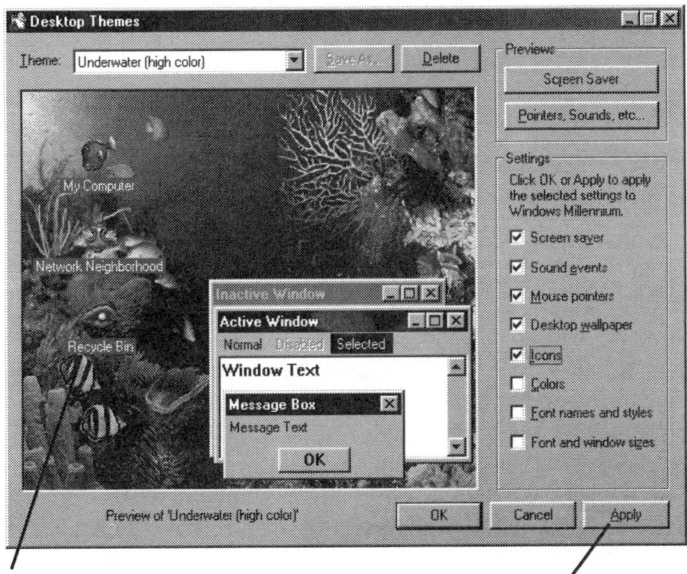

It is just as well that these icons are labelled!

Click **Apply** if you want to see the theme in place before committing yourself

IF YOU USE ALL ASPECTS OF A THEME, THE DESKTOP WILL BE MORE CONSISTENT, BUT MAY NOT BE AS CLEAR AS YOU MIGHT LIKE!

Understand fonts

A font is a typeface design, identified by a name. Within one font you will get type in a range of sizes, and the appearance may be varied by the use of bold, italic or other styles.

Fonts can be divided into three categories:

- **Serif** – like this (Garamond), have little tails (serifs) at the ends of strokes.
- **Sans serif** – like this (Arial), with simpler lines.
- Display – *decorative* fonts of all kinds.

There are thousands of fonts, and a couple of dozen of the best of these are supplied with Windows Me. You will get more with any word-processing and page layout software that you install, and you can buy CDs full of fonts. You do not need a huge number. Professional designers normally work to the 'three-font' rule: no more than three fonts on any one page, using different sizes and styles for variety and emphasis. Three or four serif and sans fonts and a dozen or so display fonts should be enough for most purposes. The more you have, the longer it will take to scroll through the font list whenever you are formatting text!

Display your fonts

1 Click **Fonts**.

2 Click to list the fonts by similarity, then choose a font from the drop-down list. If you have a lot of very similar fonts, you might think about getting rid of some.

3 Or click for large icons, or for a list display.

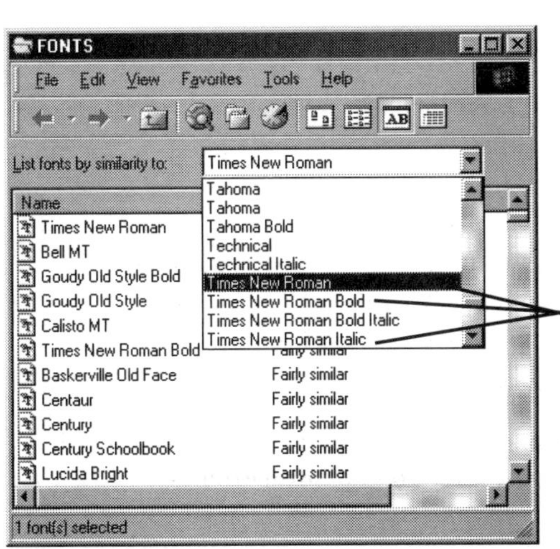

Some fonts have **Bold**, *Italic* and ***Bold Italic*** variations. Within a word-processor you will normally only see the main name in the font list – the Bold or Italic versions are then used if these effects are selected later

THE FONTS FOLDER, HERE USING THE LIST BY SIMILARITY VIEW. CHOOSE A FONT FROM THE DROP-DOWN LIST, AND THE WHOLE SET IS THEN LISTED IN ORDER OF CLOSENESS OF MATCH

View a font

1 Click **Fonts** to open the Fonts folder
2 Click the font. A viewer will open, showing samples of text in a range of sizes.
3 If you want a printed copy for closer checking, click **Print**.
4 Click **Done** or [X] to close the viewer

You can view several fonts at once if you want to compare them side by side – but note that the viewer opens in the same place on screen, so you will need to move it to see the one below

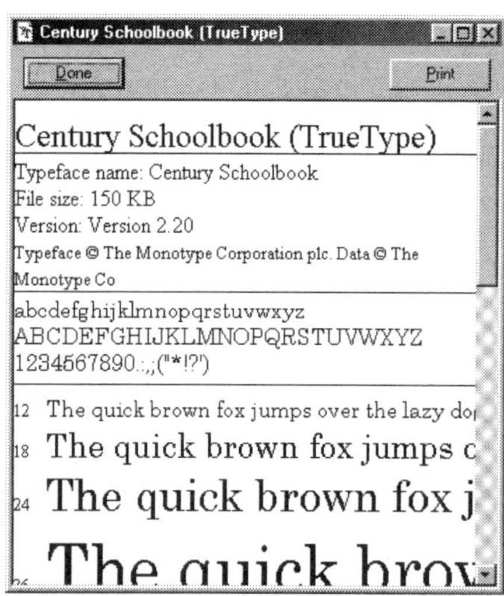

Install fonts

If you have fonts on CD-ROM or downloaded them from the Internet, they must be installed before they can be used.

1 Open the **File** menu and select **Install New Font**.
2 At the **Add Fonts** panel, select the drive and folder.
3 Select the fonts from the list, holding down **Control** while you click if you want to pick several.
4 If the font file is already on your hard disk, clear the **Copy fonts to Fonts folder** checkbox.
5 Click **OK**.

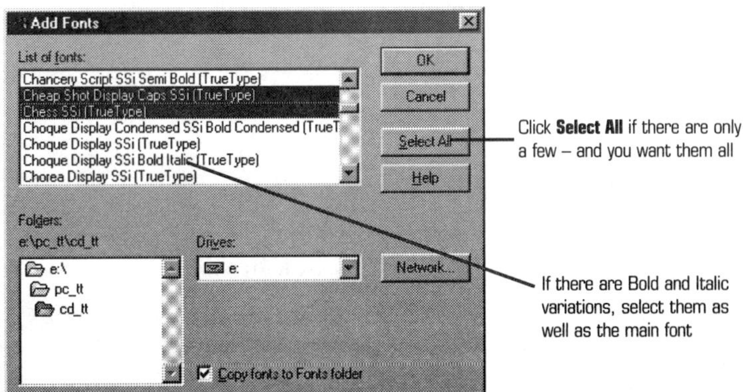

Click **Select All** if there are only a few – and you want them all

If there are Bold and Italic variations, select them as well as the main font

Adjust the keyboard

Use this panel to define how repeat keystrokes are treated. You normally want keystrokes to be picked up separately, but will sometimes want them to repeat, e.g. to create a line of ******.

- The **Repeat delay** is how long to wait before starting to repeat – if you are heavy-fingered, set this to *Long*.
- The **Repeat rate** is how fast the characters are produced. This should match your reaction times.

1 Click **Keyboard**.

2 Test the settings by typing in the test area.

3 Move the sliders to adjust the **Repeat delay** and **Repeat rate**.

4 Test and adjust until the keys respond as you would like, then click **OK**.

If you sometimes write in a different language, use the **Language** tab to set up the keyboard to toggle between two character sets

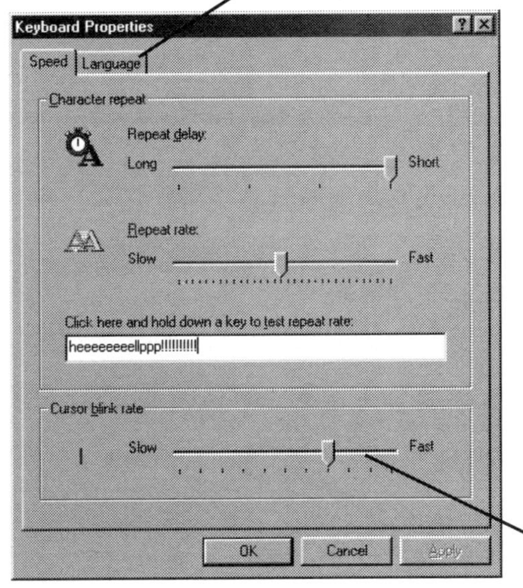

The cursor blinks when you are entering text – how fast do you want it to blink?

Configure the mouse buttons

The only crucial setting here is the **Double-click** speed – you need to be able to double-click reliably!

1 Click **Mouse** to open the panel.
2 Make sure that the **Buttons** tab is at the front.
3 Test the setting by double-clicking on the jack-in-the-box.
4 Move the slider to adjust the response if necessary.
5 Click **Apply** – not OK as we want to use the other tabs.

You can switch the buttons over if you are left-handed, but it is better to get used to the standard layout, unless this is the only PC you use and only you ever use it. (Switching to the left-handed layout will also thoroughly confuse anyone else who tries to use the machine!)

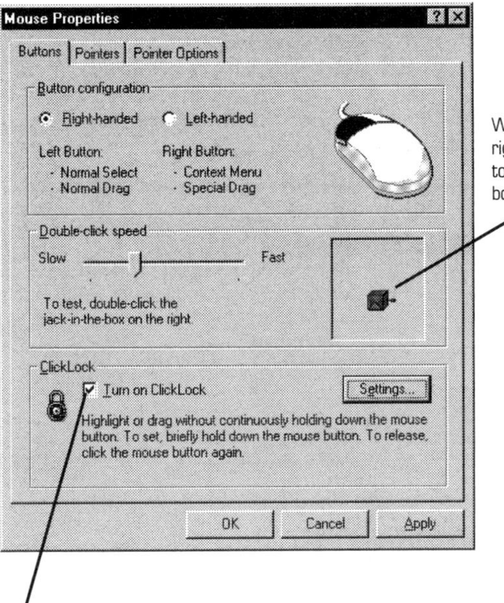

When the double-click speed is right for you, you should be able to get the jack in and out of the box effortlessly

If you find dragging difficult, try turning on ClickLock. With this on, when you need to drag something, hold down the button for a moment and it will behave as if it is being held down – click as normal to release the lock

Pick your pointers

1 Switch to the **Pointers** tab.

2 Pick a **Scheme** from the drop-down list.

3 To change a single pointer, select it and click **Browse**. You can then pick a new one from the pointers folder.

4 Click **Apply**.

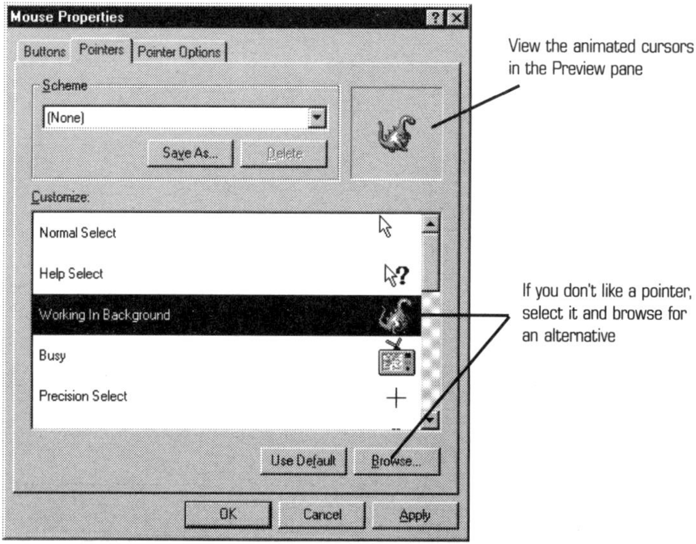

View the animated cursors in the Preview pane

If you don't like a pointer, select it and browse for an alternative

Set other pointer options

The **Pointer speed** controls how the pointer moves in relation to the mouse.

1 If you don't feel in control of the mouse, drag the slider towards **Slow**.

2 If it's taking too long to get around the screen, set it faster.

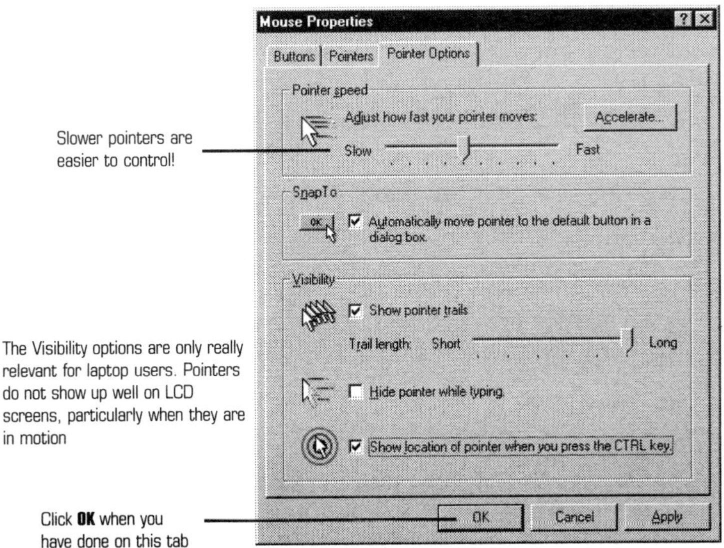

Slower pointers are easier to control!

The Visibility options are only really relevant for laptop users. Pointers do not show up well on LCD screens, particularly when they are in motion

Click **OK** when you have done on this tab

Change the sounds

Windows can attach sounds to certain events so that you get, for example a fanfare at start up and a warning noise when you are about to do something you may later regret. Some of these are just for fun; others can be very useful. If you tend to watch the keyboard, rather than the screen, when you are typing, then audible warnings can be useful.

The Sounds Properties panel is where you decide which events are to be accompanied by a sound, and which sounds to use.

1 Click **Sounds and Multimedia** 
.

2 If an event has 🔈 to its left, it has a sound attached. Click ▶ to hear the sound.

4 To change the sound, select the event and click **Browse**.

5 Click **Apply**.

The other tabs control the devices used for multimedia work. It's best to let the system sort these out.

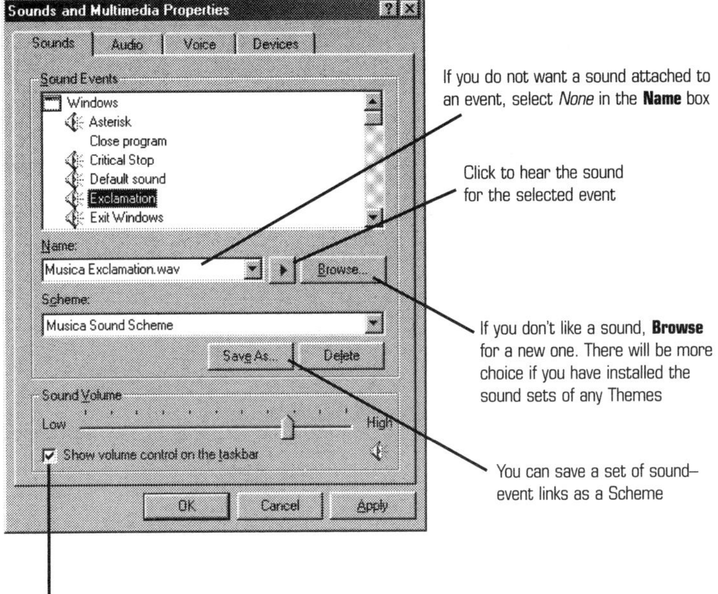

Make sure that this is ticked – if the volume control is on the Taskbar, you can change it, or switch to Mute at any time. The control shows as 🔈 in the tray on the far right

Add a user

If several people use the PC, they can all have their own personalised settings if you give them user identities.

1 Click **Users** .

2 The first time that you do this, the New User wizard will run automatically. The next time, the **User Settings** dialog box will open – click **New User…**

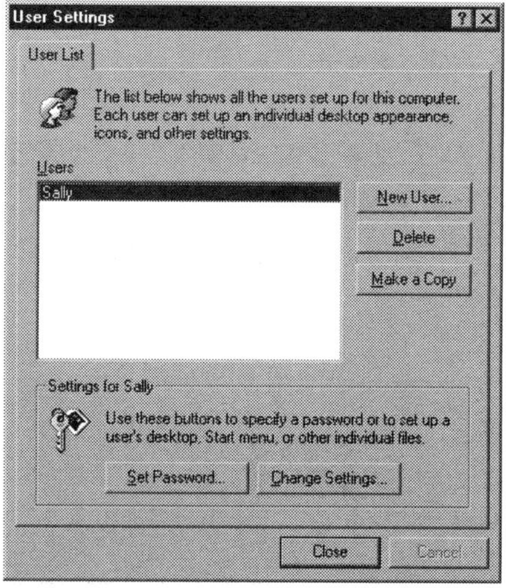

3 Enter a **User Name** and a **Password** for the person, clicking **Next** after completing each panel.

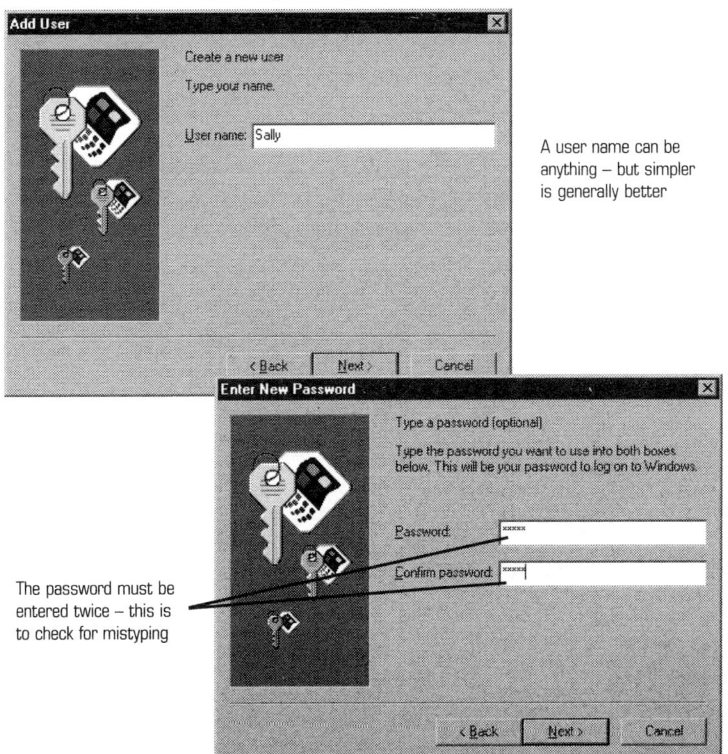

A user name can be anything – but simpler is generally better

The password must be entered twice – this is to check for mistyping

4 Select the items that you want to personalize. Users should have their own *My Documents* folder, but other items can be personalized or left common, as wanted.

5 If people have been using the PC together in the past, select **Create copies…** so they start off with the setting as they have been using them.

6 Click **Next**, then **Finish** at the following panel.

7 Wait while items are created – it can take a few minutes.

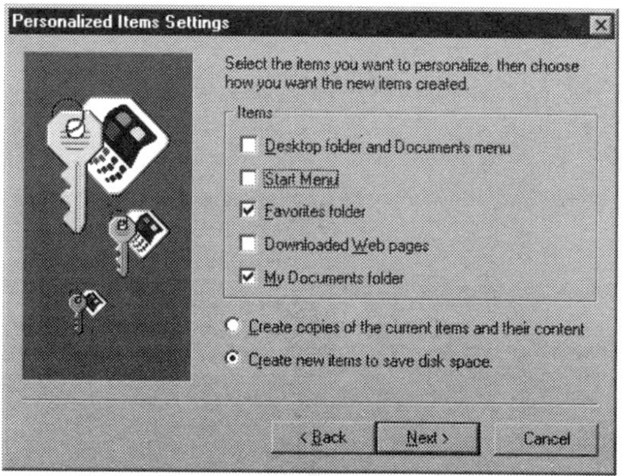

You have to restart the PC before the settings take effect.

The Taskbar and Start menu

Set Taskbar options

1 Click **Start**, point to **Settings** and select **Taskbar and Start Menu** to open its Properties panel.

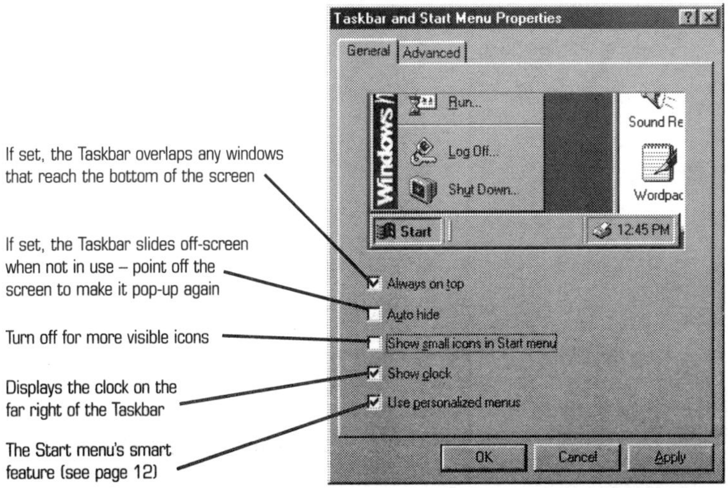

Display toolbars

In its initial settings, the Taskbar will have one toolbar on it – **Quick Launch** (see page 22). More can be added if you want to be able to start more applications from the Taskbar. There are four ready-made toolbars.

- **Address** – enter an Internet address here, and Internet Explorer will start and try to connect to it.
- **Links** – carries a set of buttons with Internet addresses: clicking one starts Internet Explorer to make the connection.
- **Desktop** – contains copies of the icons present on the Desktop.
- **Quick Launch** – for starting the main Internet applications.

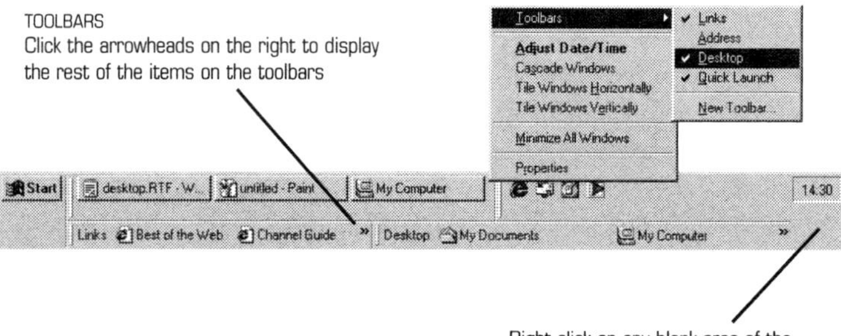

THE TASKBAR WITH THE LINKS AND DESKTOP

Change a toolbar's options

The short menu that can be opened from a toolbar contains the usual Taskbar items, plus some options for the toolbar. Most of these are at the top of the menu.

View > **Large** or **Small** sets the icon size.

Show Text adds labels.

Refresh simply redraws the toolbar.

Open opens the toolbar's folder so that you can add or remove shortcuts.

Show Title displays the toolbar's title.

Close closes the toolbar – you will be prompted to confirm this.

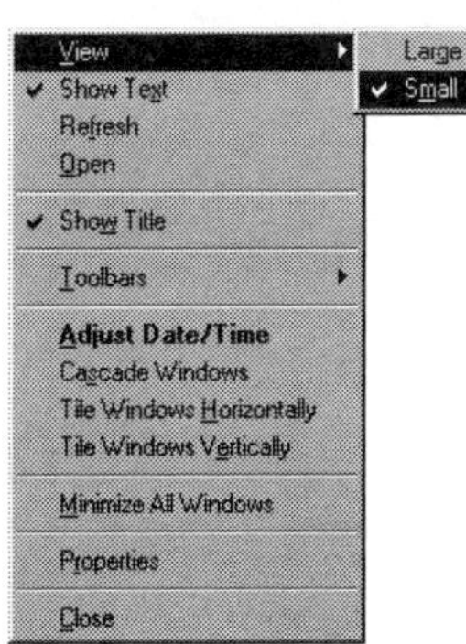

Create a toolbar

You can set up your own toolbars with shortcuts to applications, folders or Internet links:

1 Create a folder, within My Documents, and name it 'My Tools' or something similar.

2 Set up shortcuts to your applications or folders (see page 94).

3 If you are going to show text labels on the toolbar, edit the names so that they are as brief as possible.

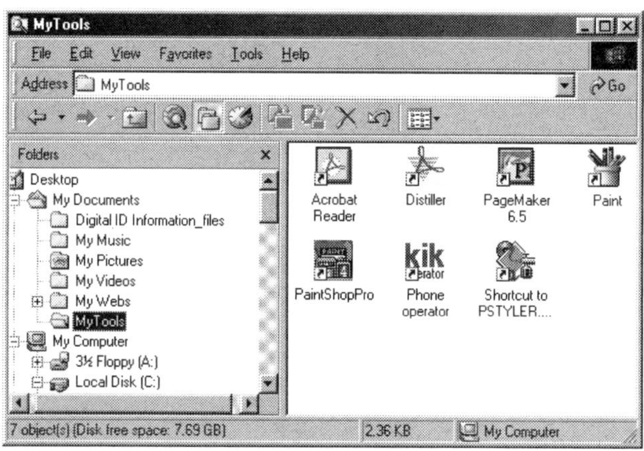

THE NEW TOOLBAR FOLDER, ALMOST READY TO BE ADDED TO THE TASKBAR – THE PHOTOSTYLER SHORTCUT NAME NEEDS EDITING

4 When you have assembled your shortcuts, right-click on the **Taskbar**, point to **Toolbars** and select **New Toolbar...**

5 Work through the folder display to find the one containing your shortcuts.

6 Click **OK**.

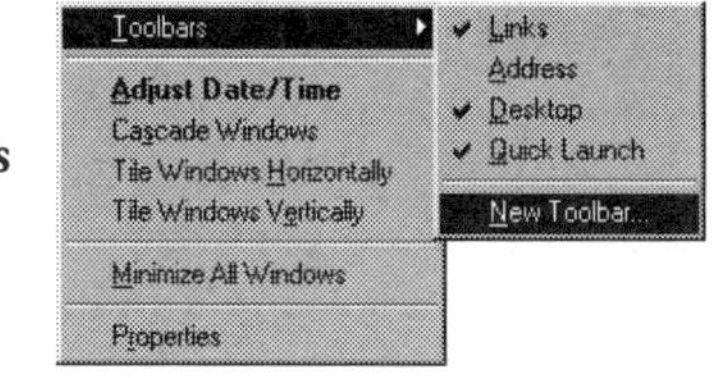

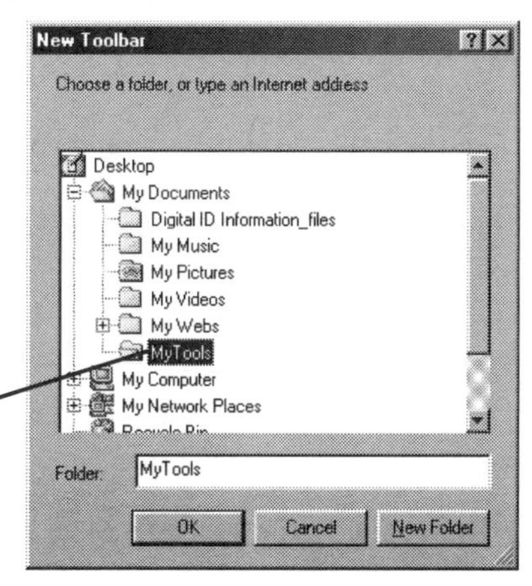

Browse to the new toolbar folder

Resize the Taskbar

The Taskbar is normally a thin bar across the bottom of the screen, which is fine when it is used only for the Quick Launch toolbar and a few application buttons. Add more toolbars and it is going to get crowded and difficult to use.

One possible solution is to make the Taskbar deeper by dragging its top edge upwards.

The toolbars can be rearranged within this area by dragging on their handles. Move them up or down between the lines, or drag sideways to adjust their relative sizes.

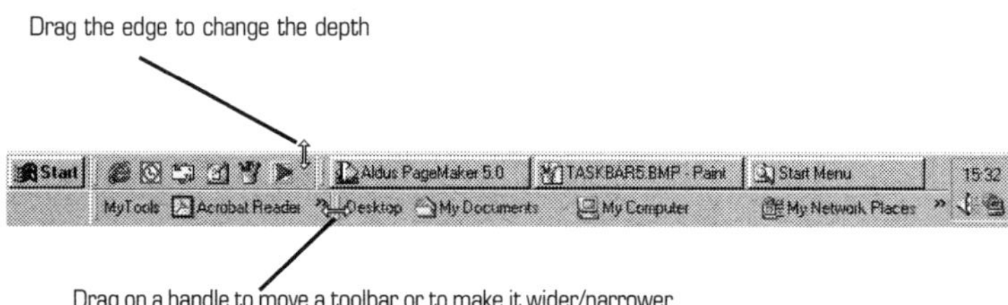

Move the Taskbar

A second solution is to move the Taskbar to one or other side of the screen. By default it will be wide enough to show the Text labels on the icons.

1 Click onto the Taskbar in the space to the right of the application buttons.
2 Drag the Taskbar up to the side.
3 Drag on the handles between the sections to adjust the layout.
4 Drag the edge inwards if you want to make the bar slimmer.

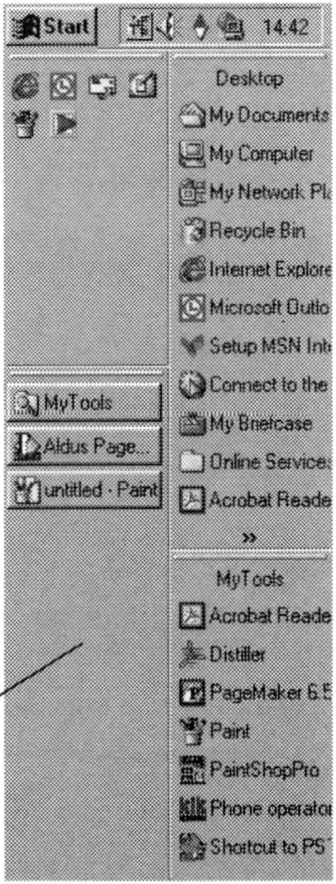

Click into this space to drag the Taskbar

Add entries to the Start Menu

If you switch to the **Advanced** tab of the **Taskbar and Start Menu Properties** panel, you can control which items appear on your menu system, and where they appear.

Adding an entry is a fiddly job, but fortunately not one that you have to do very often – with most software, the setup routines normally add the Start menu entries for you.

1 Click **Add**. This will start a wizard to guide you.

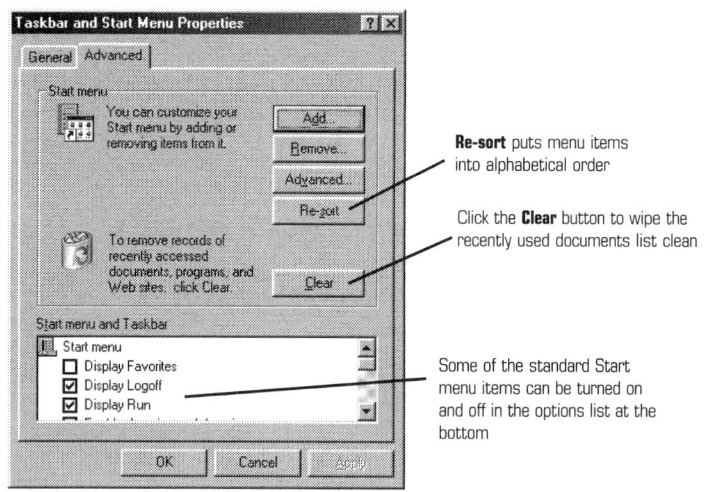

Re-sort puts menu items into alphabetical order

Click the **Clear** button to wipe the recently used documents list clean

Some of the standard Start menu items can be turned on and off in the options list at the bottom

2 At the **Create Shortcut** stage, click **Browse** and locate the program file. Click **OK**, then click **Next** at the wizard panel.

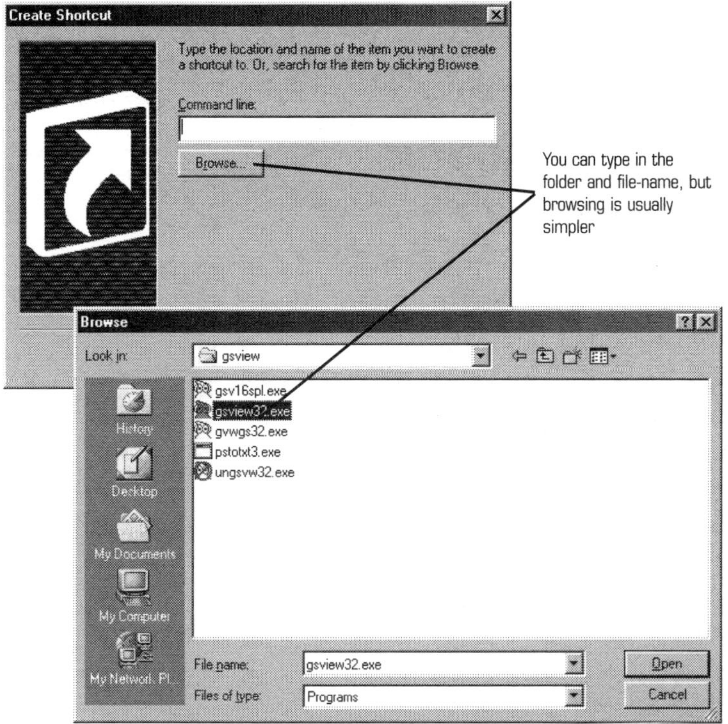

You can type in the folder and file-name, but browsing is usually simpler

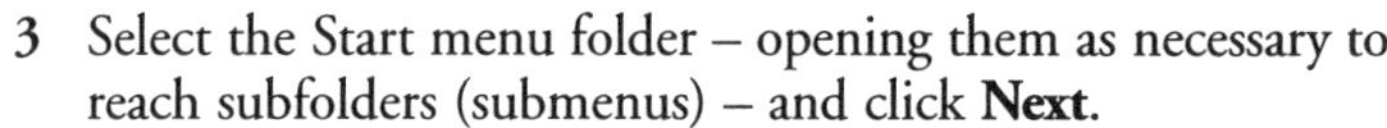

3 Select the Start menu folder – opening them as necessary to reach subfolders (submenus) – and click **Next**.

4 Finally, type a name for the menu item and click **Finish**.

The menus are presented as folders – open them as needed to reach the right place

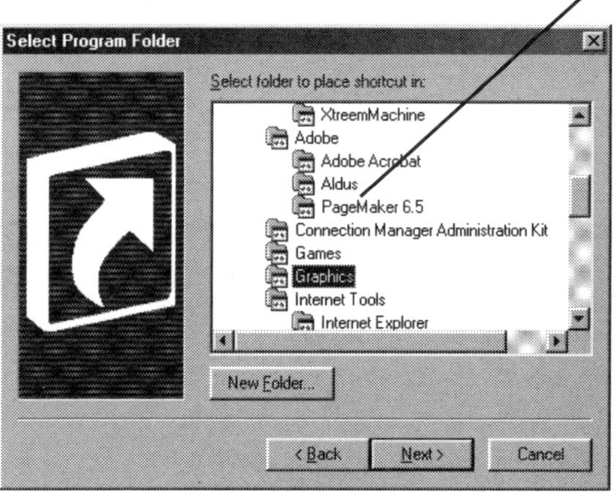

Remove an entry

Some setup routines don't just put in entries for the applications; they also create shortcuts to the 'Readme' file (that you may read once) and to the Help pages (that you only open from within the application). Some uninstall routines fail to clear the entries from the Start menu when the program is removed. Some software creates duplicate entries in the main menu and in submenus.

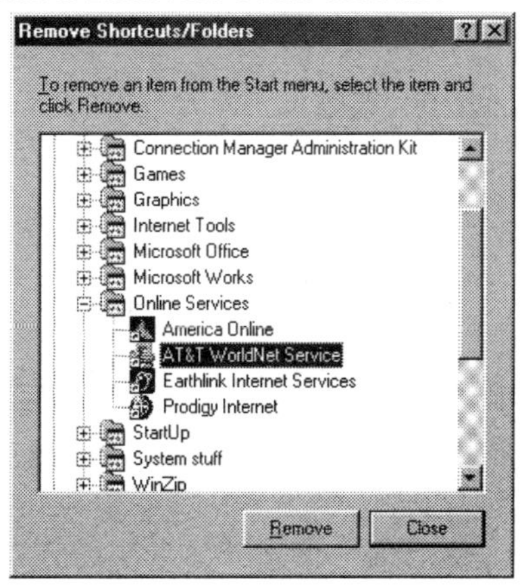

1 At the **Start Menu Programs** tab, click **Remove.**
2 Open up the folders (submenus) as necessary.
3 Select the item and click **Remove.**
4 Click **Close.**

Tip

Whole folders can be removed if desired.

Reorganize the menus

The Start menu system is stored as a set of folders and subfolders in the *C:\Windows\Start Menu* folder. You can open it in Windows Explorer or My Computer, though it is probably simpler to click the **Advanced** button on the **Start Menu Programs** tab. This opens a limited version of Windows Explorer. You cannot move up out of the Start Menu folder, but all the normal file management techniques for moving, deleting and renaming files and folders work here.

Tip

If you have installed so many applications that your Start menu has become overcrowded, create 'group' folders and move the entries and folders of related applications into these. A short main menu that leads to two or three levels of submenus is much easier to work with than one huge menu!

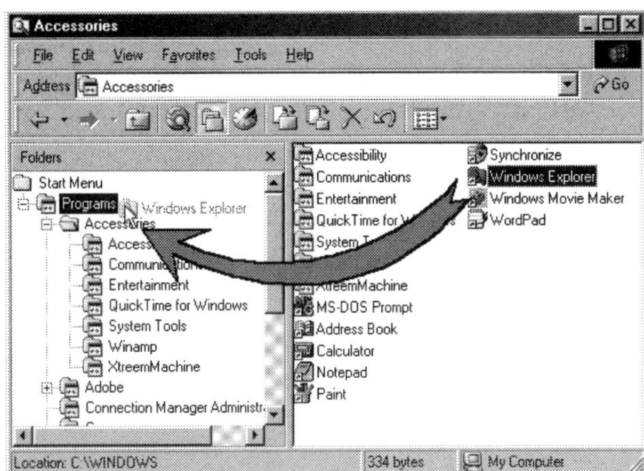

THE **ADVANCED** BUTTON LETS YOU EXPLORE THE START MENU. IN THE EXAMPLE, WINDOWS EXPLORER IS BEING MOVED FROM THE *ACCESSORIES* TO THE MAIN *PROGRAMS* MENU – SUCH A USEFUL PROGRAM SHOULD BE EASY TO GET TO

MANAGING YOUR PC

Printers

Add a printer

If your printer dates from before Spring 2000, the drivers – the programs that convert computer files into the right form for printing – on the Windows Me CD are probably newer than those supplied with the printer. If it is more recent, dig out its installation disk.

The **Add Printer Wizard** makes installation simple.

1 Open the **Printers** folder, from the **Start → Settings** menu.

2 Click (or double-click) **Add Printer** to run the wizard.

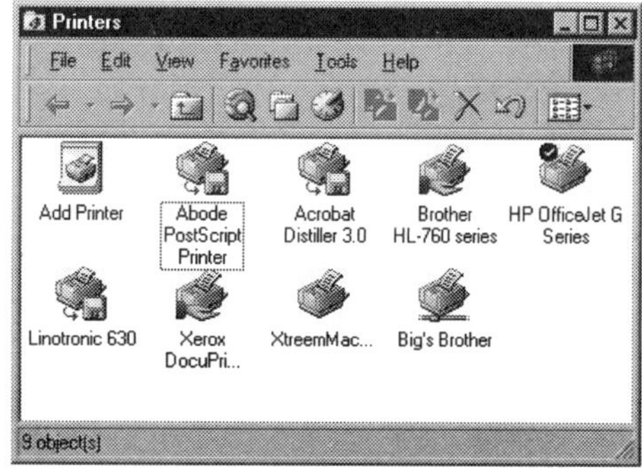

This system has several printers – the OfficeJet is the default (shown by ✔); Big's Brother is on the network

3 At the first screen, select *Local printer*, if it is attached to your PC, or *Network printer* if you are on a Network and the printer is attached to another PC.

4 If you are using a Windows driver, select the **Manufacturer** from the list, then the **Printer** model. If you are using the drivers supplied with the printer, click **Have Disk**, then select the model from the list that is drawn from the disk.

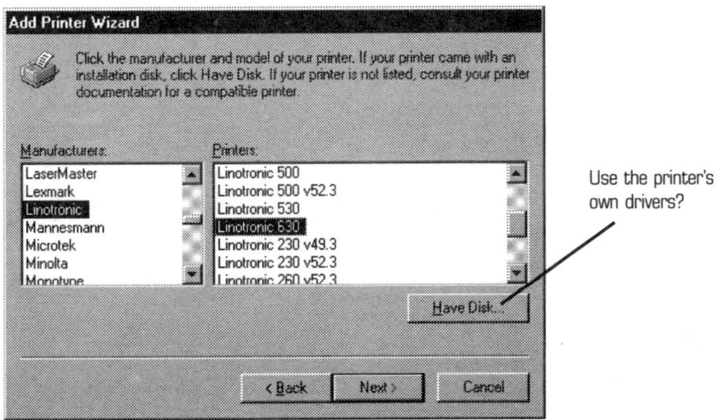

5 For a local printer, you need to choose the port – normally LPT1.

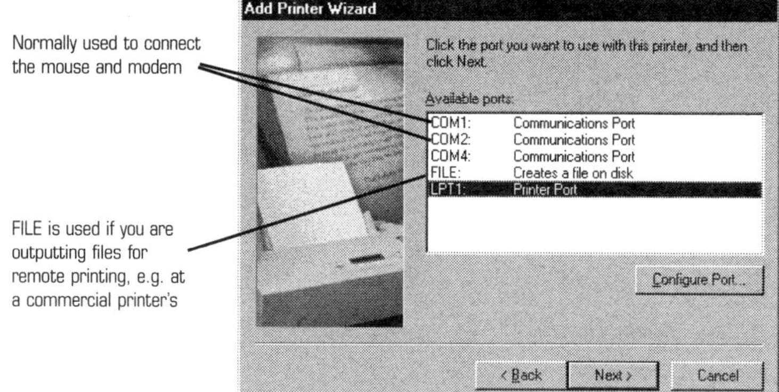

6 For a network printer, browse the network to find the printer you want to use.

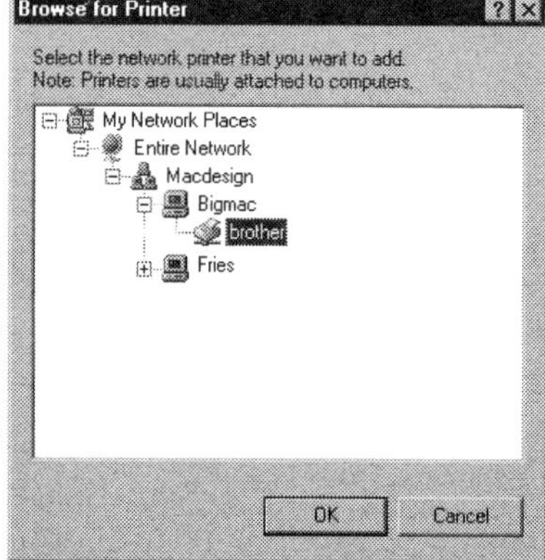

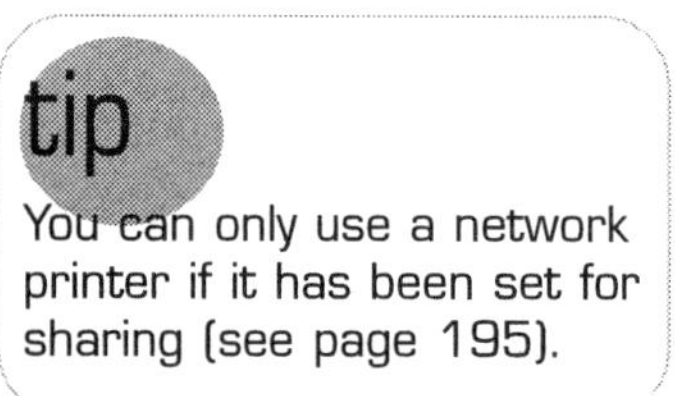

tip

You can only use a network printer if it has been set for sharing (see page 195).

7 You may want to edit the full manufacturer/model name into something shorter to label the icon in the Printers folder.

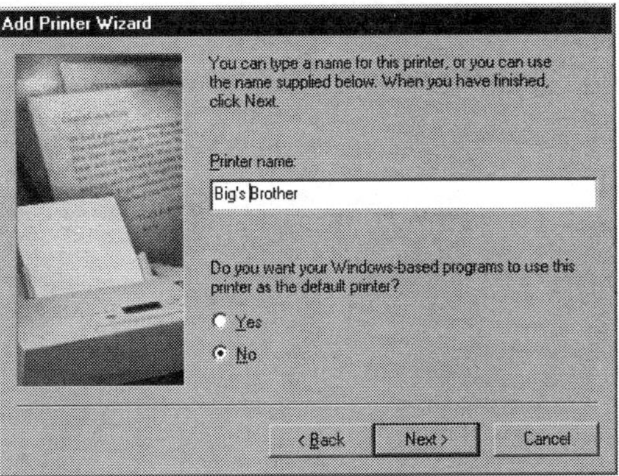

8 At the final stage, accept the offer of a test print – it's as well to check! Once you click **Finish**, the Wizard will load the driver from the disk and install it in your system.

Set the default printer

If you have more than one printer attached to your system, one of them must be set as the default. This is the one that applications will use unless you specify otherwise.

1 Open the **Printers** folder.

2 Right-click on the printer.

3 Select **Set as Default**.

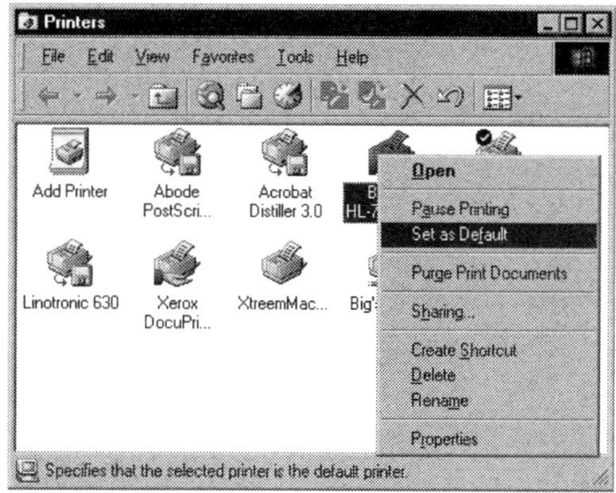

tip

If you click a program's Print button to print something, it will be sent to the default printer. To choose the printer, you must work through the Print dialog box (see page 159).

Printer properties

Right-click on the icon in the Printers folder and select **Properties**. Different printers have different panels, but you should find:

- A **General** tab, where you can type a comment – this may be useful on a network.
- A **Paper** tab, where you can set the default paper size – the standard UK size is A4. The other options here are best left at their defaults. You can change them just before printing a document – the properties can be accessed from the Print routines of applications.

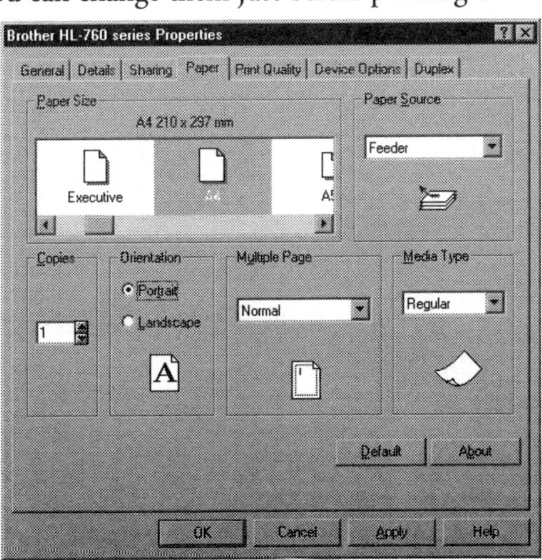

- A **Details** tab, where you can select a new port or driver if needed. The **Timeout** settings define how long Windows should wait before reporting an error; the **Spool** settings determine whether the file is sent directly to the printer, or through a memory buffer. Spooling frees up applications, as they can send data out faster than the printer can handle it.

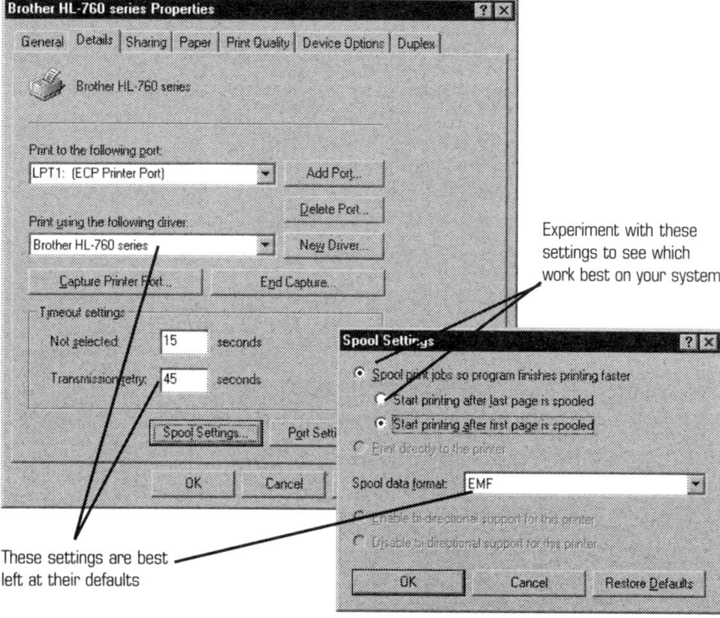

- Colour printers will have at least one tab where you can fine-tune your colour mixes.

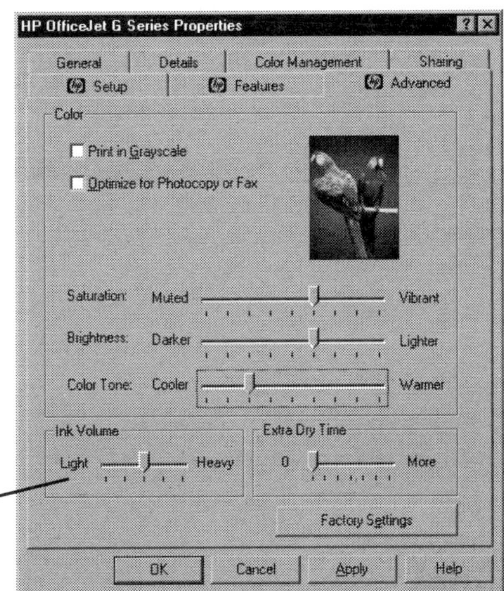

The same colour settings can have different effects on different types of paper – experiment and observe!

If you normally print one or more draft copies to check before the final print, set the ink volume (or toner level) low

These are only the default settings, and they can be changed, from within an application, before printing a document.

Print from within an application

The Print routines in applications are all much the same. There will usually be a toolbar button, and clicking on this will send the document to the printer using its current settings – whatever they are.

The first time that you print something, it is best to start by selecting **Print** from the **File** menu. This will open a dialog box where you can define the settings. The key settings are which pages to print and how many copies.

tip

If you need to change the layout, print quality or other printer settings, click the **Properties** button to open the printer Properties panel – this may look slightly different from the panel opened from the Printers folder, but gives you access to the same settings.

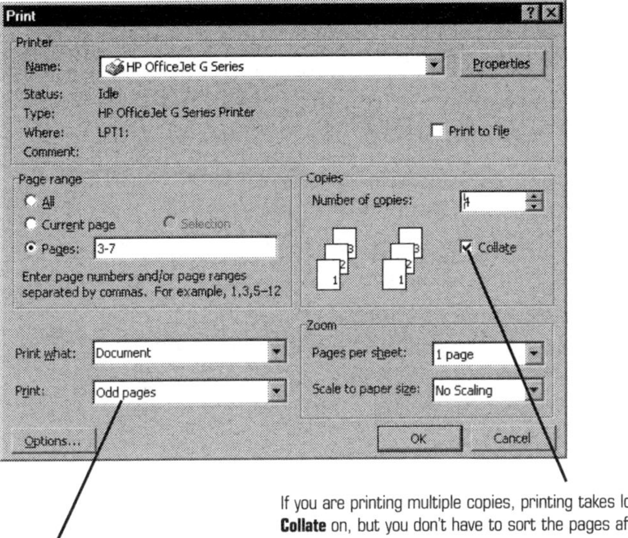

If you are printing multiple copies, printing takes longer with **Collate** on, but you don't have to sort the pages afterwards

For double-sided printing, print the Odd pages first, then put the paper back in, turn on Reverse printing (it's on Word's options) and print the Even pages

THE PRINT DIALOG BOX FROM WORD. OTHER APPLICATIONS HAVE DIFFERENT OPTIONS, BUT **PAGE RANGE** AND **COPIES** ARE COMMON TO ALL

Control the print queue

When a document is sent for printing, it goes first to the print queue. If it is the only print job, it is processed directly. If not, it will sit in the queue and wait its turn. As long as a document is in the queue, you can do something about it.

- If you discover a late error, so that printing would be just a waste of paper, a job can be cancelled.
- If you have sent a series of documents in succession, you can change the order in which they are printed.

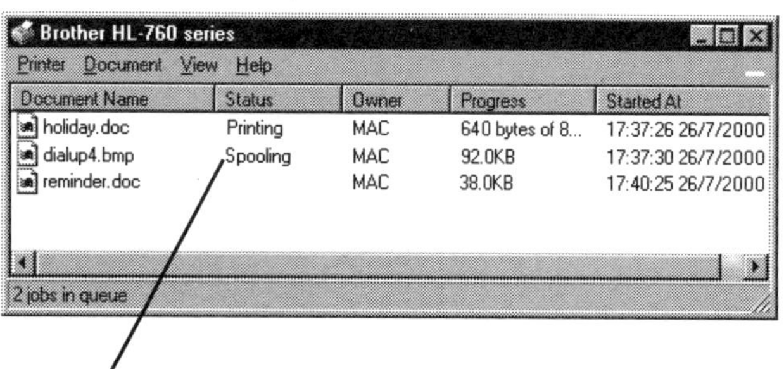

You can cancel a document after it has started printing, but you can only change the positions of documents lower down in the queue

When the printer is active, you will see [printer icon] on the right of the Taskbar, next to the clock. Click on it to open the printer's folder, where the queue is stored.

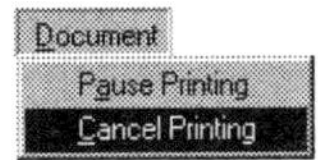

- *To cancel a print job*, select the document, then use **Cancel Printing** from the **Document** menu.

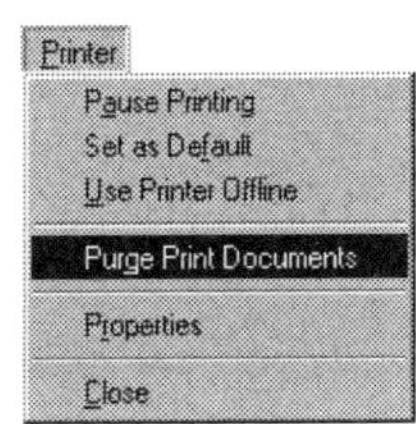

- *To cancel all the queued jobs*, use **Purge Printing** from the **Printer** menu.
- *To change the order of printing*, select a document and drag it up or down the queue as required – this only works with those documents that are not already being spooled or printed.

tip

As printers can store some pages in their own memories, printing may continue for a while after you have cancelled a job. The only solution is to turn off the printer – but don't do this while a sheet is part-way through or you'll cause a jam.

Print a document from its file

If you have Windows Explorer or My Computer open, you can print a document directly from there, as long as you have an associated application which can handle it. Windows Me will open the application, print the document, then close the application for you.

To send the document to the default printer:

- Right-click on the file and select **Print** from the short menu.

To send to any other printer:

1 Open the Printers folder and arrange the screen so that you can see the document file and the printer icon.

2 Drag the document across the screen and drop it onto the printer icon.

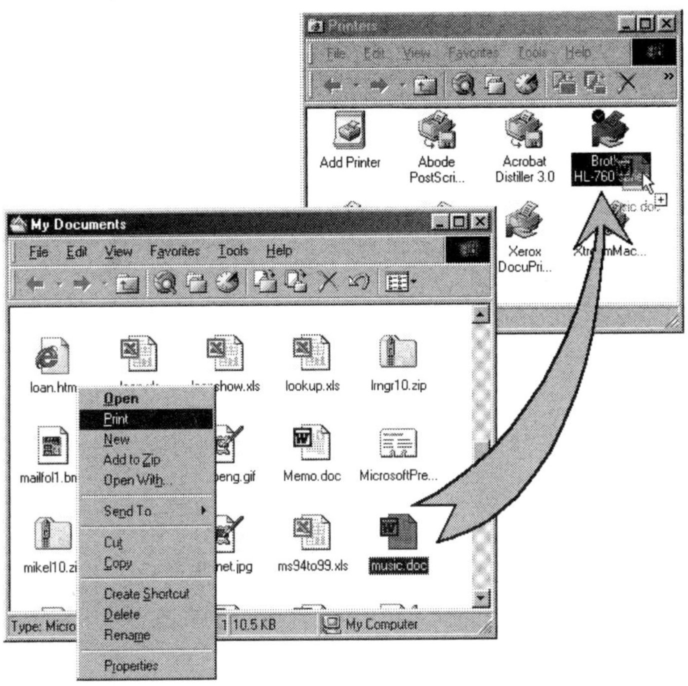

YOU CAN PRINT A DOCUMENT DIRECTLY FROM ITS FILE, EITHER FROM THE SHORT MENU OR BY DROPPING IT ONTO A PRINTER ICON

Housekeeping

Find the System Tools

These can be reached from the **Start** button, through **Programs → Accessories → System Tools**. Open the **System Tools** menu and see what's there. You may well have a slightly different set from the one shown here.

Disk Cleanup, Disk Defragmenter and Scandisk – the main disk management tools – can also be run from a disk's Properties panel, or automated with the Maintenance Wizard. Get to know these, as well-maintained disks are essential for a reliable system.

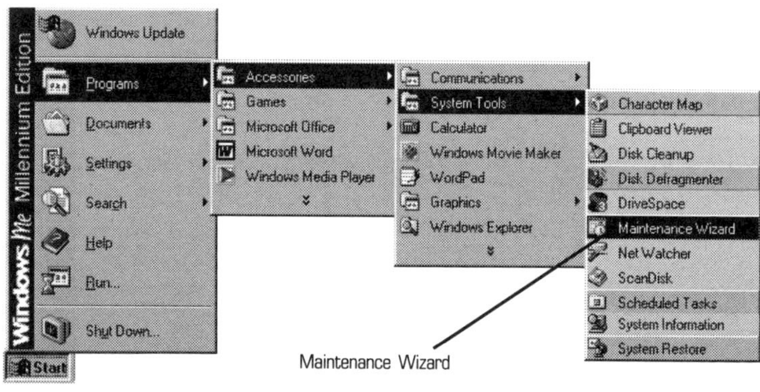

Disks and drives

These words are often used interchangeably but, strictly speaking, a disk is that flat, round thing on which data is stored, while a drive is a logical area of storage identified by a letter (A:, C:, etc). The A: drive can have different disks put into it. A hard disk can be 'partitioned' to create two or more drives.

A disk – hard or floppy – is divided into *clusters*, each of which can contain all of a small file or part of a larger one. When a file is first written to a new disk, it will be stored in a continuous sequence of clusters, and the disk will gradually fill up from the start. If a file is edited and resaved – bigger than before – it will overwrite the original clusters then write the remainder in the next available clusters, which may well not be physically next to them on the disk. When a file is deleted, it will create a space in the middle of the used area, which later may be filled by a part of another file. Over time disks get messier, with files increasingly stored in scattered clusters. A file that is held in one continuous chunk can be opened much more quickly, simply because the system does not have to chase around all over the disk to read it.

View a disk's properties

If you right-click on any drive in My Computer, and select **Properties** from the menu, its Properties panel will open.

- The **General** tab shows how much used and free space you have on the drive.

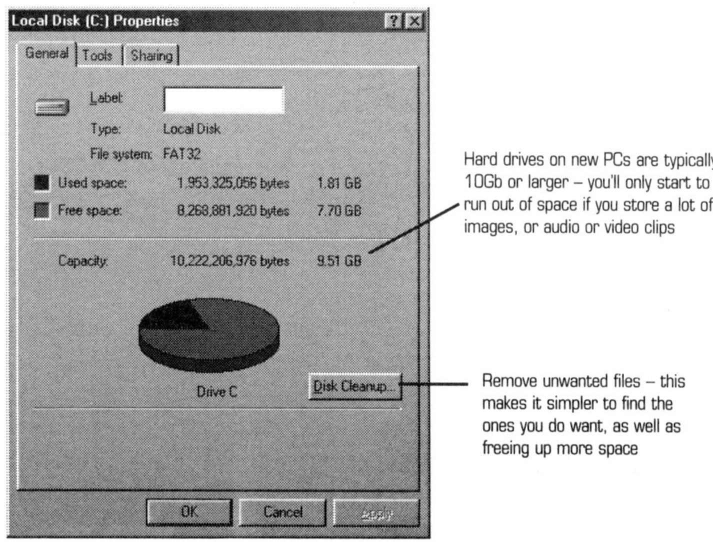

Hard drives on new PCs are typically 10Gb or larger – you'll only start to run out of space if you store a lot of images, or audio or video clips

Remove unwanted files – this makes it simpler to find the ones you do want, as well as freeing up more space

- The **Tools** tab has buttons to start ScanDisk and Disk Defragmenter.
- The **Sharing** tab is only present if you are on a network (see page 196).

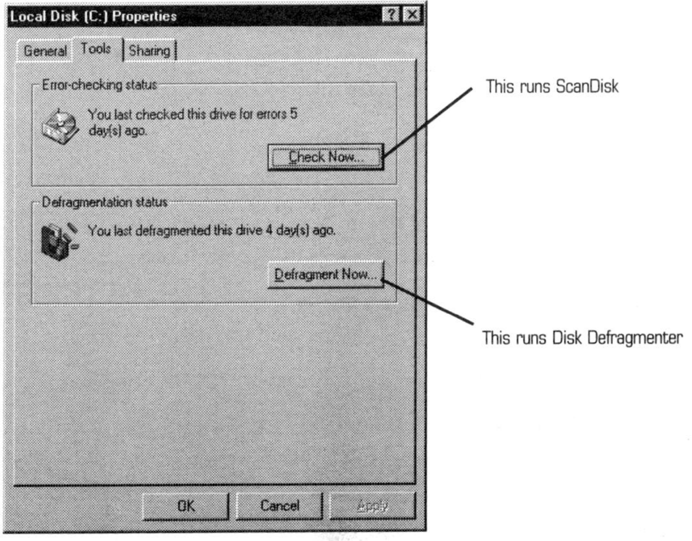

Clean up a hard disk

This removes temporary and other unwanted files from the hard disk. Run it regularly to free up space and keep the clutter down.

1 Start **Disk Cleanup**, either from the **System Tools** menu or the **General** tab of the **Properties** panel.

2 Select the drive – normally **C:**.

3 Select the sets of files to delete. The key ones are:

- **Temporary Internet Files** – don't remove these if you will be revisiting pages, or you will have to download them again.
- **Downloaded Program Files** refer to applets from Web pages that were stored on your disk so that they could be run.
- **Offline Web Pages** – pages that were downloaded and stored for reading offline. (See *Quick Fix Internet Explorer 5.5*.)
- **Recycle Bin** – saves you having to empty the Bin separately.
- **Temporary Files** refers to those created by applications, such as automatic backups and print files. They are normally cleaned up when the application is closed, but may be left behind if it ends with a crash. Disk Cleanup will not touch any of today's files, which the application may still be using.

- **Temporary PC Health Files** are surplus copies of files used by the System Restore routines (page 182) and can be cleared.

4 Click **OK.** You will be prompted to confirm the deletions – they are irreversible – before the cleanup starts.

The **More Options** tab takes you to **Add/Remove programs**; on **Settings** you can opt to run Disk Cleanup automatically if you get short of space

Tick the ones to remove

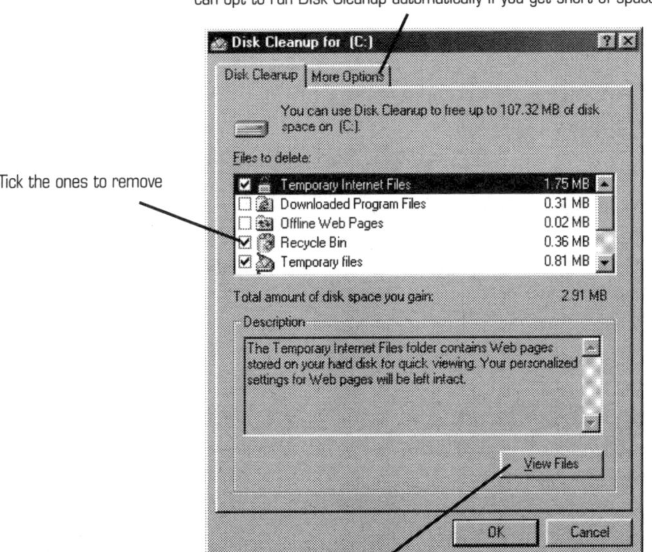

If you are not sure, check the files before marking the set for deletion

Check a disk for errors

ScanDisk will find and fix errors on a disk.

- A **Standard** scan checks that all files and folders are where they are supposed to be, and takes only a few minutes.
- A **Thorough** scan also checks that the disk surface is sound, and that data can be written to and read from it correctly. Use this when first checking a disk or after significant errors have been shown by a Standard check. It can take an hour or more!

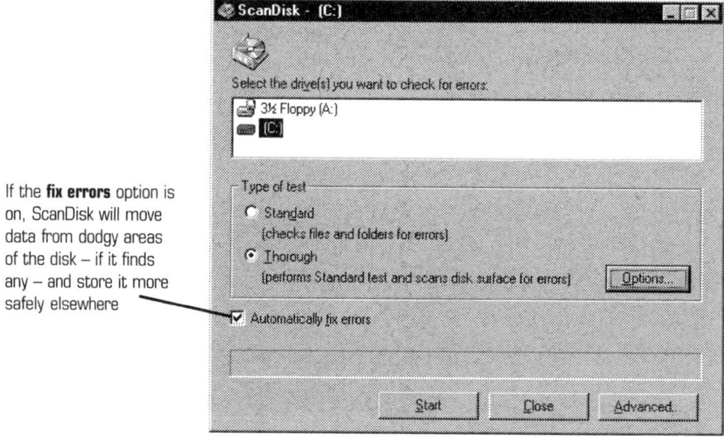

If the **fix errors** option is on, ScanDisk will move data from dodgy areas of the disk – if it finds any – and store it more safely elsewhere

The Thorough Options

A Thorough scan can be controlled through the **Options**.

- Hidden and system files cannot be repaired as this involves moving them, and these files normally have to be in a set place. This is unlikely to be a problem, as these files are largely protected by the System Restore routines (see page 182).
- Write-testing checks the disk surface, but adds significantly to the total time.

Files in the System area cannot normally be moved – they must be at set locations. If there are errors here, and System Restore cannot deal with them, it may be time for a new disk

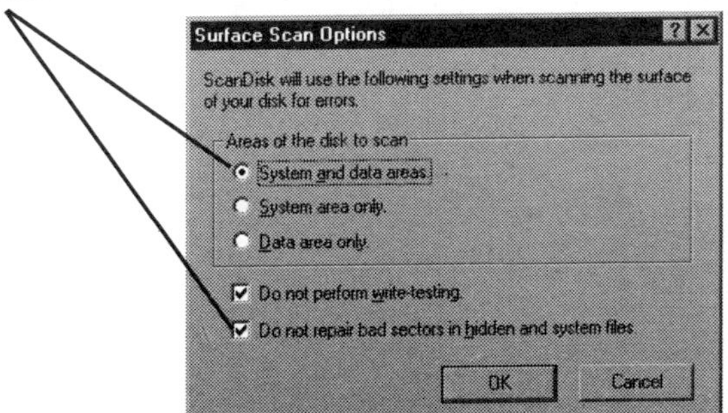

The Advanced Options

These apply to all scans. The key options here are:

- **Lost file fragments** – data-filled clusters that are no longer linked to their files. They can be converted to files (named FILE001.CHK, FILE002.CHK, etc., and stored in C:\). If the data is text it may be possible to recover it from here by opening the files in a word-processor.
- **Cross-linked files** – where the same data is linked to two files. The data can only belong to one of the two – and may belong to neither. Making a copy may leave one of the files intact.

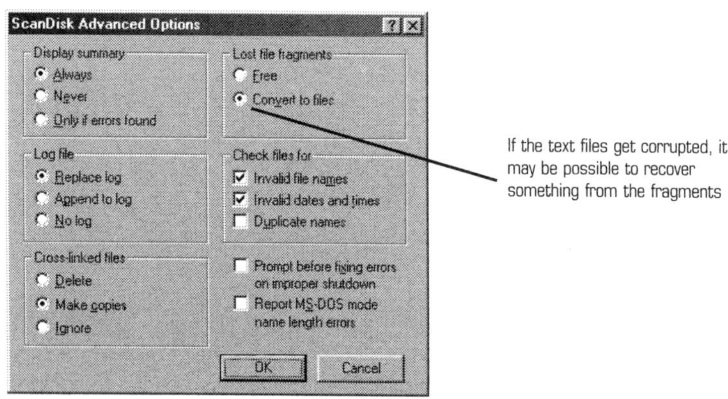

If the text files get corrupted, it may be possible to recover something from the fragments

Defragment your disks

Disk Defragmenter reorganizes the physical storage of files on the disk, pulling together the data from scattered clusters. Though it improves performance, the gains are in the order of a few seconds for starting a program or loading a data file, and it is a very slow job – allow an hour or more on a 10Mb disk. It is only worth doing regularly if your disk is well over half full – so that new files are being stored in a limited area – or if you have a high turnover of files from working on large databases or reports, or from installing and removing demos, shareware and other programs.

1 If a program writes to the disk while Disk Defragmenter is running, it will restart from scratch. Close any applications that may create temporary files – this includes the screensaver, so turn that off through the Desktop's Properties panel.

2 Start Disk Defragmenter from the **System Tools** menu.

3 Select the drive and click the **Settings** button.

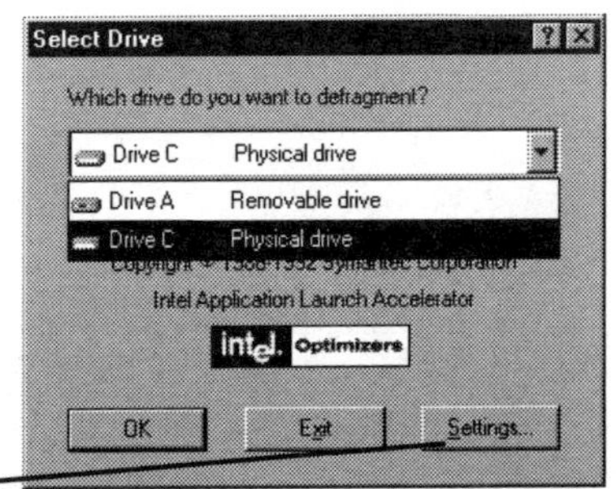

Check the Settings

4 If you have scanned the disk recently, clear the **Check for errors** option to save time.

5 Click the **Show Details** button if you want to see what's going on, then turn on the **Legend** so that you can understand it!

6 When you get bored, go and do something else for an hour.

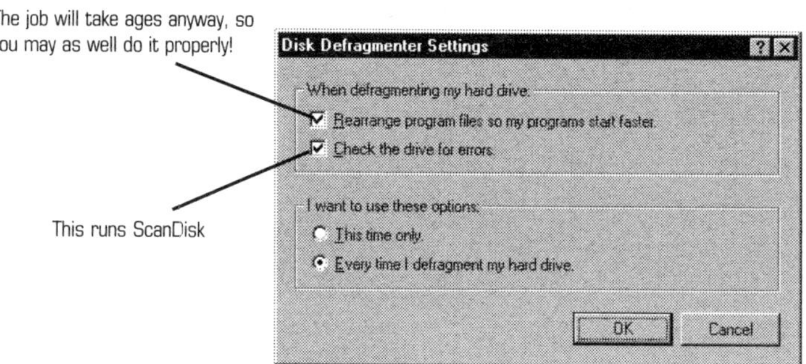

If a floppy disk becomes corrupted so that you cannot read its files, try running it through ScanDisk then Disk Defragmenter. This will sometimes recover the lost files.

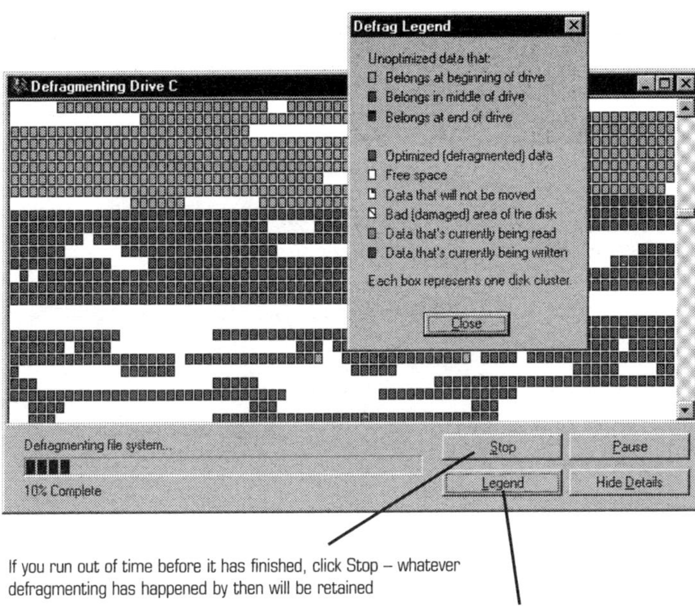

If you run out of time before it has finished, click Stop – whatever defragmenting has happened by then will be retained

It's worth watching Defragmenter at work – for a little while – just to see what it does. Turn on the legend if you want to make sense of the display!

Run the Maintenance Wizard

Disk Cleanup, ScanDisk and Disk Defragmenter can be set to run automatically. Whether you are doing it for the first time, or checking and adjusting the settings, use Maintenance Wizard.

1 Start the **Maintenenance Wizard** from the **System Tools** menu.

2 At the first panel, select **Express** to let Windows make the decisions, or **Custom** if you want to control what's going on.

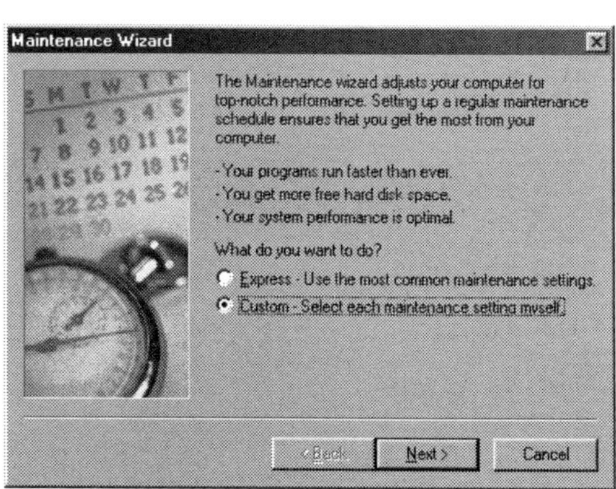

Use **Custom** to set your own times and options – it only takes a couple of minutes to work through the Wizard

3 Pick a time when you will not be using the PC. If you have chosen the Express route, click **Finish**, otherwise click **Next**.

Maintenance Wizard

Select a Maintenance Schedule

Windows can perform maintenance tasks only when your computer is on.

The easiest way to maintain your computer is to leave it running all the time, and schedule maintenance to happen at night.

When do you want Windows to run maintenance tasks?

Nights - Midnight to 3:00 AM

Days - Noon to 3:00 PM

Evenings - 8:00 PM to 11:00 PM

Custom - Use current settings

< Back | Next > | Cancel

Remember that **Cleanup** and a standard **ScanDisk** only take a few minutes

4 If there are programs in your Startup folder – i.e. ones that run when Windows starts – you will be asked if you want to run them.

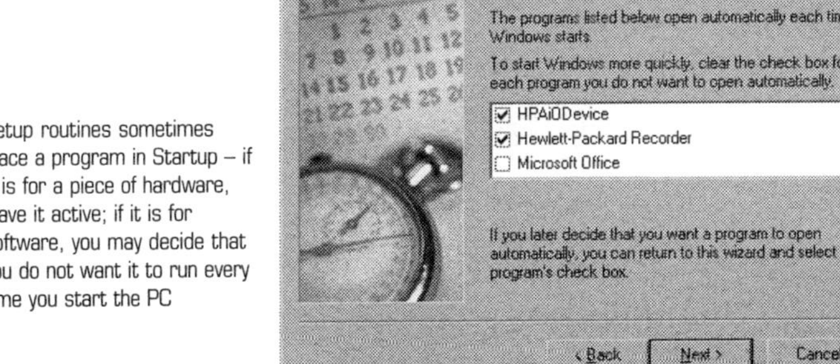

Setup routines sometimes place a program in Startup – if it is for a piece of hardware, leave it active; if it is for software, you may decide that you do not want it to run every time you start the PC

5 You will see a panel for each of Disk Defragmenter, ScanDisk and DiskCleanup. All follow the same format. If you choose to run the utility, you can change when and how often it runs by clicking **Reschedule**, and set its options by clicking **Settings** – this leads to the utility's normal options panel.

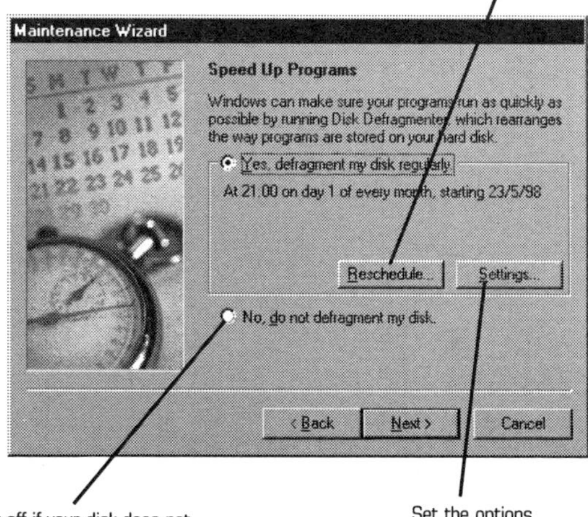

Set the times/intervals

The tools can be run at different times and intervals – and you don't have to run them all

Turn it off if your disk does not need defragmenting regularly

Set the options

6 When rescheduling, the first stage is to decide the frequency – which will vary with the job and your usage pattern. You then specify which day of the month or week, and the time of day.

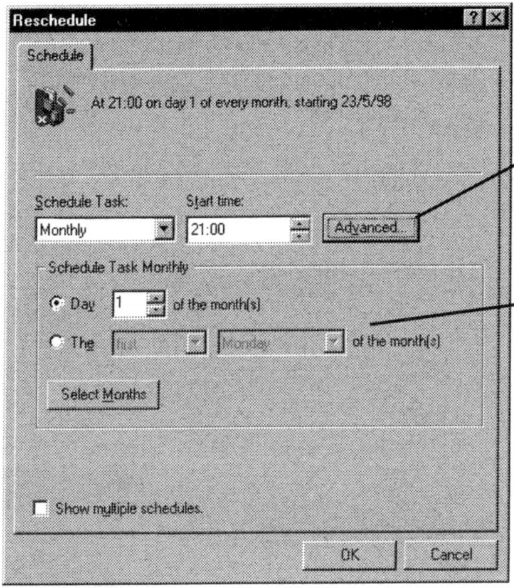

Lets you set repeat rates and stop time

This part of the panel varies to suit the basic interval – daily, weekly, monthly and others

tip

If a job cannot start at the scheduled time, it will try later, unless you turn this option off (see next page).

Control your Scheduled Tasks

After the Maintenance Wizard has been run, the settings are stored in the **Scheduled Tasks** folder, which can be opened from the **System Tools** menu. Click on an icon here to enable or disable a task, or to change its schedule or settings.

To disable a scheduled task:

Clear the **Enabled** checkbox at the bottom of the **Task** tab.

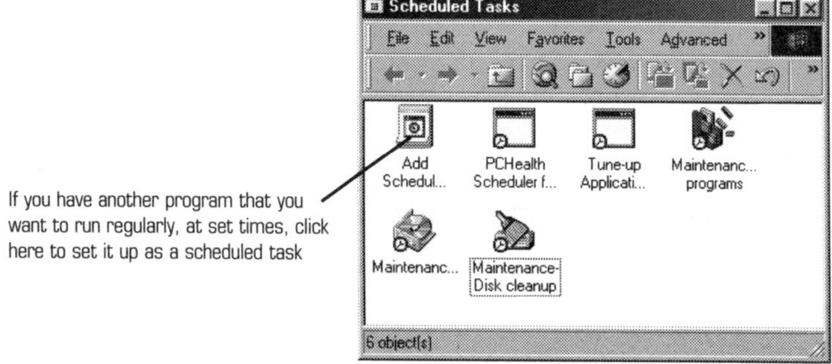

If you have another program that you want to run regularly, at set times, click here to set it up as a scheduled task

THE SCHEDULED TASKS FOLDER. CLICKING AN ICON OPENS ITS CONFIGURATION PANEL – IT DOES NOT START THE TASKED PROGRAM

You will not want your scheduled tasks to interfere with your use of the computer. Scheduling the tasks for times when the PC will be on, but not in active use – e.g. lunchtime – will help, but the occasional clash may still occur. The **Settings** tab lets you define the interaction between the task and your work.

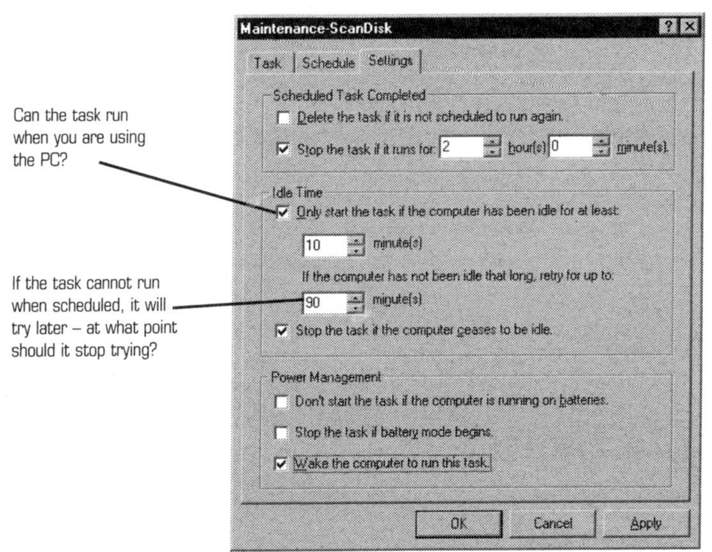

Restore your system

With any luck you'll never need System Restore, but it's good to know that it is there. Windows Me stores a backup copy of the key system files, known as *system restore points*, at regular intervals. If the files become corrupted, perhaps by 'user error' or when installing software, this will get your PC running again.

1 Go to the **System Tools** menu and select **System Restore**.

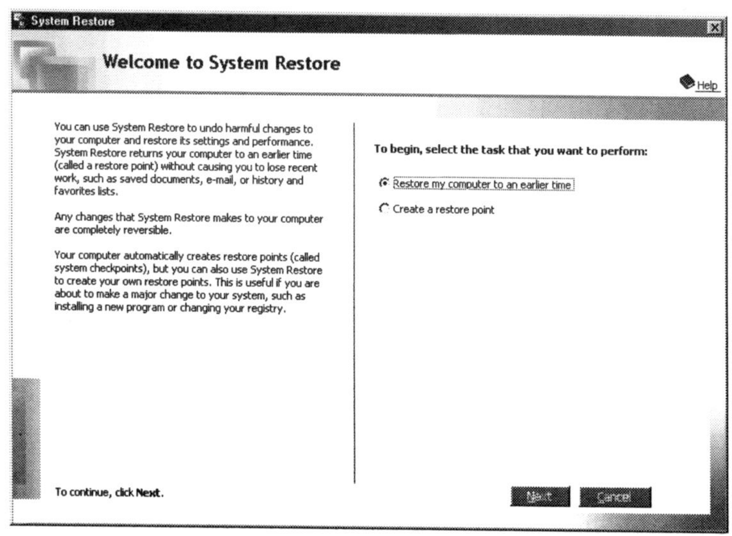

2 At the first stage, select **Restore my computer…**

3 At the next panel, pick the most recent checkpoint when you know that the system was running properly, and click **Next**.

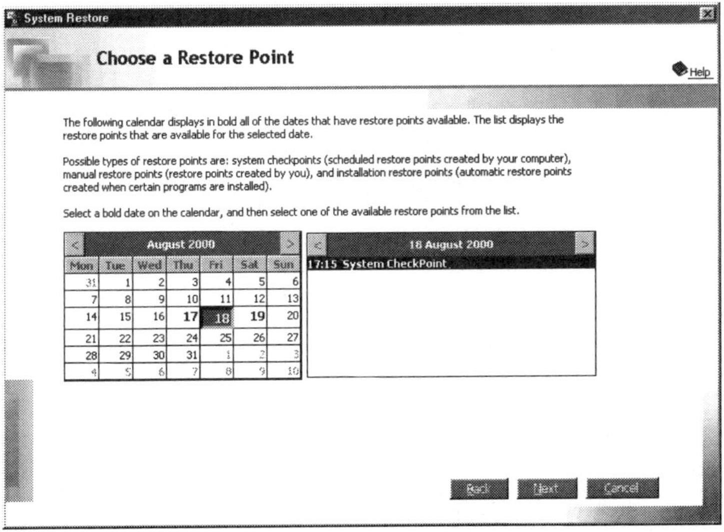

System Restore

Choose a Restore Point

Help

The following calendar displays in bold all of the dates that have restore points available. The list displays the restore points that are available for the selected date.

Possible types of restore points are: system checkpoints (scheduled restore points created by your computer), manual restore points (restore points created by you), and installation restore points (automatic restore points created when certain programs are installed).

Select a bold date on the calendar, and then select one of the available restore points from the list.

August 2000

Mon	Tue	Wed	Thu	Fri	Sat	Sun
31	1	2	3	4	5	6
7	8	9	10	11	12	13
14	15	16	**17**	**18**	**19**	20
21	22	23	24	25	26	27
28	29	30	31	1	2	3
4	5	6	7	8	9	10

18 August 2000

17:15 System CheckPoint

Back Next Cancel

4 You will be prompted to shut down any programs and save any open files before setting the operation running. System Restore is irreversible. Only run it if you need to!

Create a restore point

A Windows Me computer is robust; modern software and hardware is normally reliable and thoroughly tested, but things do go wrong. Before you do anything which might upset the system, such as installing new kit or making any other major changes, you should create a restore point. This will ensure that there is a current copy of the system files – it may have been a few days since the last system restore point was created.

1 Start **System Restore** and select **Create a restore point**.

2 Type in a description to help you identify it – the point will have the date and time added, so this is not too crucial.

3 Click **Next** to start the process.

It takes only a few minutes to create a restore point and it could save you endless hours of pain!

Format a floppy disk

These are mainly used for backups and for copying files from one PC to another. Before use they must be formatted – this creates a structure on the magnetic surface of the disk, marking it off into storage areas. New disks can be bought ready-formatted. If not, you will have to format them. It only takes a few moments.

1 Place an unformatted disk in the floppy drive.

2 Right-click on the **A:** icon in My Computer and select **Format...** from the menu.

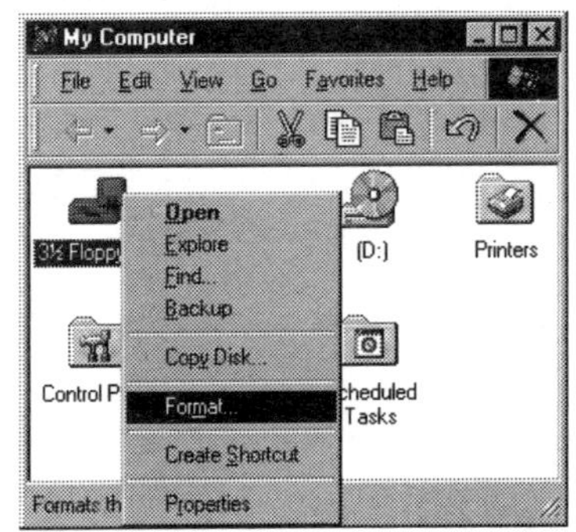

tip

Formatting destroys all the data on a disk. **Do not format the C: drive!** The option is there, but it should only be used as a last-ditch attempt to recover something from the ruins of a total failure – and only ever with professional advice.

3 At the **Format** dialog box, in **Format Type**, select *Full.*

4 Type a **Label** if wanted – the paper label is more use for identifying floppies.

5 Click **Start**.

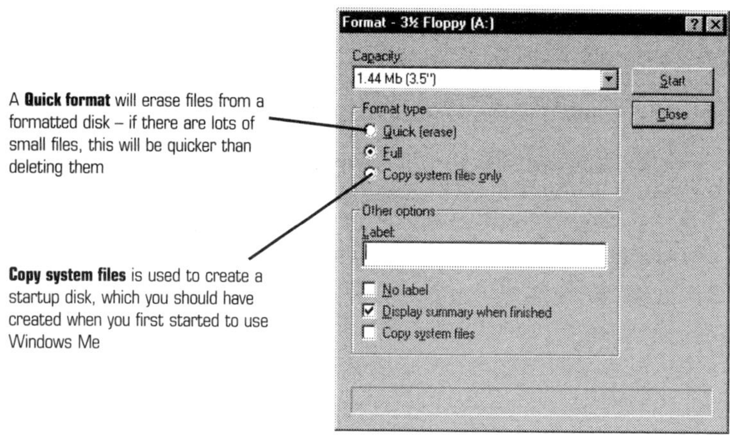

Networking

Set up a home network

Setting up even a small network used to be a real chore, but the Home Networking Wizard has transformed the business. It is so easy to use – with two provisos.

- Networking is quite straightforward as long as you are just connecting Windows Me PCs together. You can also connect to Windows 98 PCs, but you won't get quite the full range of facilities through the link. If you want to share an Internet connection, the PC with the modem must be an Me PC.
- You still have to open the PCs' boxes and install the network cards, and their software, then cable them together. This is not difficult. If you can use a screwdriver, hammer in cable clips (or secure the cable in some other way) and follow instructions, you should be able to set up your network hardware.

The Wizard must be run on each PC. They can be set up, individually, at any time, but it's probably simplest to do all the PCs in one session.

Set up network hardware

There are so many variations here that it is not possible to give any detail of how to do it – the hardware should, in any case, come with detailed instructions for its installation. What follows is just general guidance. You need to understand a little about networking, then look at the PCs and their locations, before going to your dealer to see what they can supply to meet your requirements.

In a typical small network, each PC has a network adapter card, and the PCs are joined by thin co-axial cable. To set this up, each PC must have at least one empty expansion slot.

- There are two varieties of expansion slots – PCI and ISA. Older PCs have ISA slots; newer ones have PCI or a mixture of both. Check your PC's documentation to see what it has, then open the case to see if any are empty. Adapter cards also come in PCI and ISA varieties and must match the slots, though you can have PCI cards in some computers and ISA cards in others.

If you do not have empty slots, there are networking systems which work through the USB ports.

You will need one length of cable between each pair of PCs. Any computer dealer should be able to supply you with cables with their connectors fitted and in suitable lengths. (Measure along the actual cable run – not the direct distance – between each pair of PCs. If the dealer does not make up cable to order, then longer is OK – the spare can be coiled out of the way.) The cable should be fitted securely, so that it can't be trodden on or tripped over.

- If there is no convenient, safe or visually acceptable way – you do not want cable looped across the living room ceiling – to run cable between your PCs, it is possible to connect through the electrical mains circuits. (A method which is safer and more practical than it sounds at first!)

Network adapters and cables are designed to work at a range of speeds. If you are mainly using the network to share access to the modem and a printer, then a basic 1Mb network will do the job. If it is going to be used for playing high-speed networked games, you will want something faster.

Once you have a clear idea of what sort of network can be installed on your system, and what you want to use it for, go to your local dealer and talk to their network specialist.

Run the Home Networking Wizard

The Wizard handles all the details of setting up the networking software. You just need to tell it a little about your system, and decide the PCs' names and which folders and printers to share.

1 From the **Start** menu, go to **Programs** → **Accessories** → **Communications** and run the Wizard.

2 At the Internet Connection stage, tell it if you want to use the Internet from that PC and whether it is has the connection.

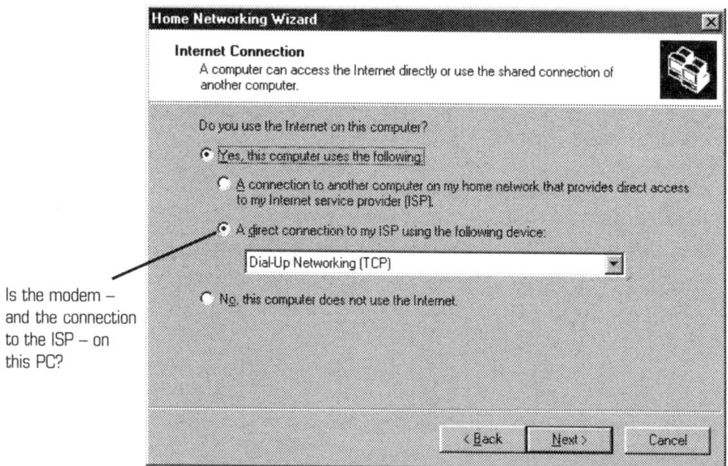

Is the modem – and the connection to the ISP – on this PC?

3 On the PC with the modem, select Yes to let the networked computers use it.

4 Give names for the computer and the workgroup. The names are entirely up to you, but should be single words, and keeping them simple and easy to remember is always a good idea. In a home or small office, all PCs would normally be in the same workgroup.

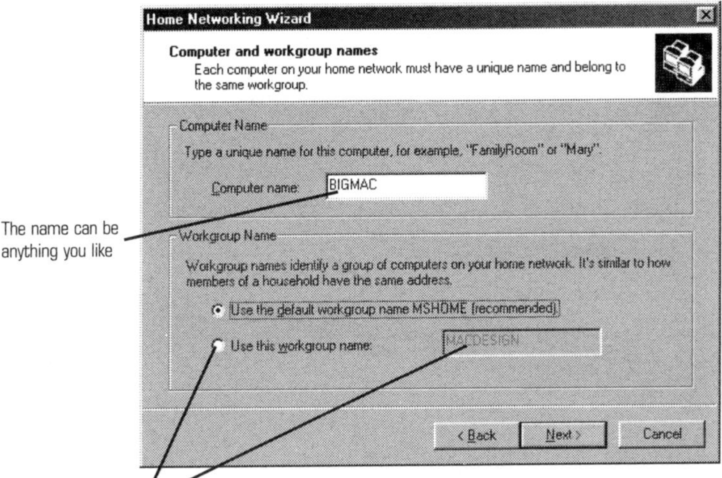

5 At the **Share** panel, tick the checkboxes if you want other computers to have access to the PC's *My Documents* folder and its printer.

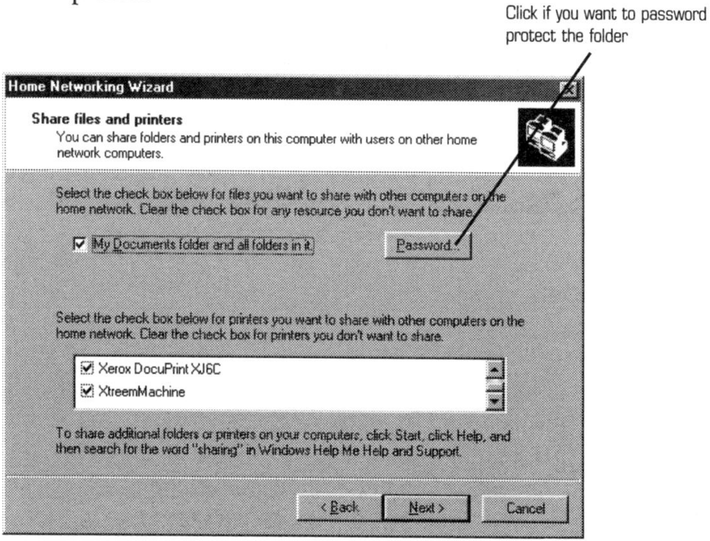

tip

Once the network is in place, you can fine-tune the access to the folders and printers (see *Share resources*, page 194).

6 If one of the PCs is running Windows 95 or 98, you will need a special **Home Networking Setup disk**. You will be offered the chance to create one before the Wizard closes.

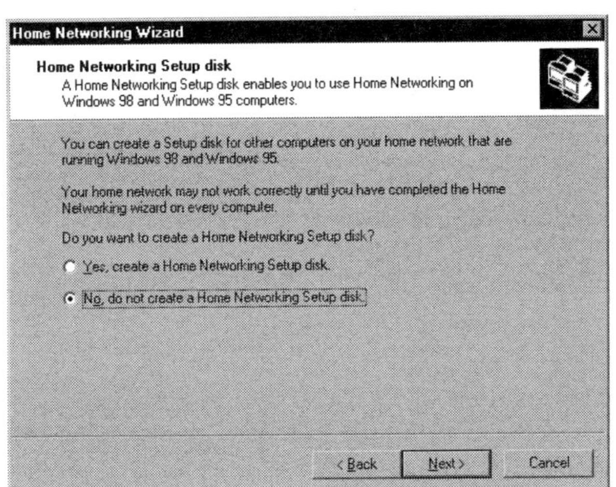

7 Click **Finish** at the final panel and wait a few minutes for the Wizard to do its stuff. The PC must be restarted afterwards.

Share resources

You can change the level of access that other users have to the folders and printers on a PC at any time. These changes take effect immediately.

A folder can be shared in two ways:

- *Read-only* will allow other users to read the files or run the programs that are stored there, but it will not let them edit or delete files, or store new files.
- *Full access* allows other users to treat the folder as if it were on their own PC.

At either level, access can be controlled by a password.

If you share a drive, all its folders are initially shared in the same way. You can then adjust the share level on individual folders, but this can only be to give *greater* access – not *less*. If a disk is shared at full access, then every folder within it is fully shared.

- If you only want others to have access to selected folders, set the disk to **Not Shared**.

Share a printer

1 Open the **Printers** folder from the **Start → Settings** menu.

2 Right-click on the printer and select **Sharing…**

3 Turn Sharing on or off.

4 Click **OK**.

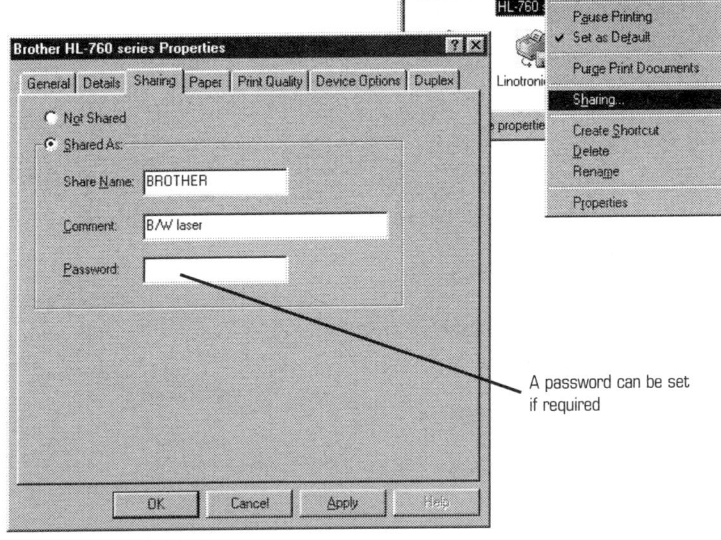

Share folders

1 Run Windows Explorer or My Computer.

2 Right-click on the folder and select **Sharing…**

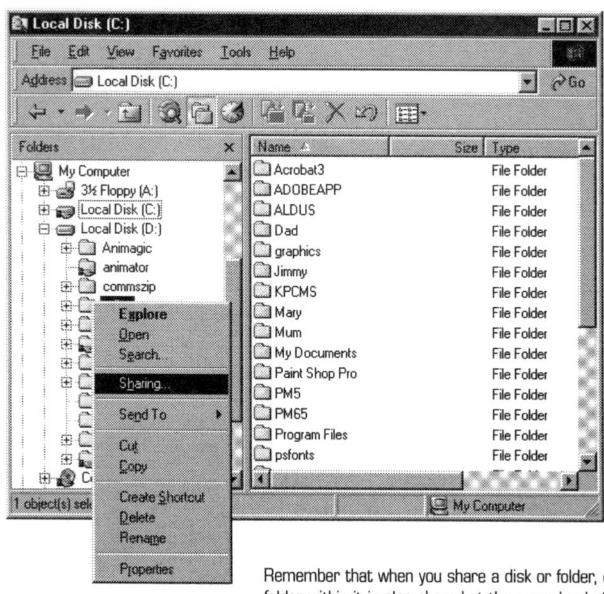

Remember that when you share a disk or folder, every folder within it is also shared at the same level of access

3 Set the **Access Type** to **Read-Only**, **Full** or **Depends on Password**.

4 For password controlled access, set passwords for *Read-Only* and for *Full* access – they can be the same or different, or one or other left blank.

5 Click **OK**.

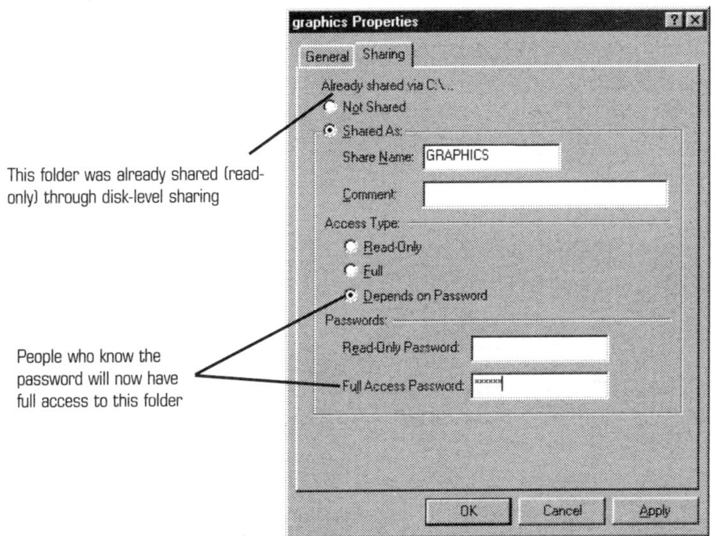

Explore My Network Places

Once the network is set up, use **My Network Places** to view the other PCs' shared drives – it works just like My Computer.

1 Open **My Network Places** from the Desktop.

2 Click on a folder to open it.

3 Open files as normal.

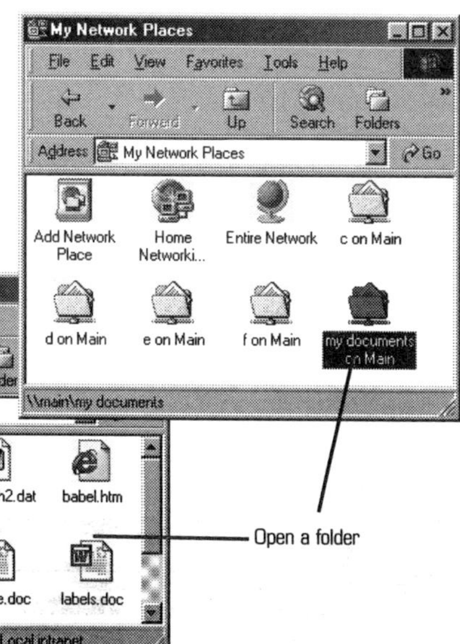

Use older applications on the network

New Windows software can handle network connections with no trouble. When you want to open or save a file, it will let you reach across the network and link to any shared folder. Older applications were often not designed for use on networks, and will only allow you to reach files on drives on the same PC. Windows Me has a neat solution. You can *map* networked drives – assign drive letters to them. The C: drive on the PC in the study, for example, which might have a network name of //Study/ C/ could then be referred to as F:/ by the PC in the living room.

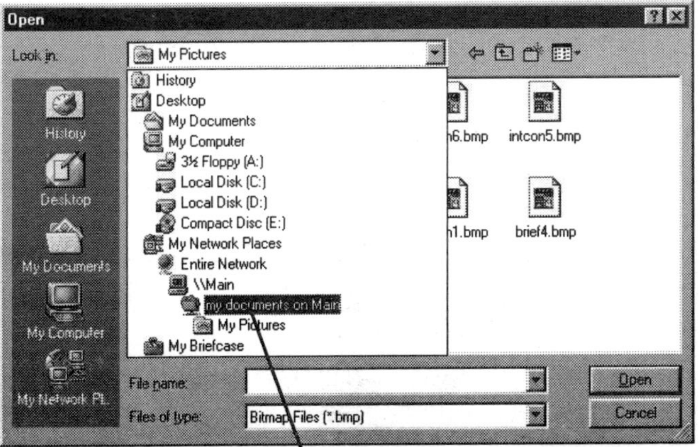

In the new Open and Save dialog boxes, you can reach the network through the **Look in** folder display

Map drives

A drive is mapped once, at the start of a session, from Windows Explorer or My Computer and can then be referred to by its assigned letter by any application.

1 Run **Windows Explorer** or **My Computer**.

2 Right-click on the drive you want to link to and select **Map Network Drive…**

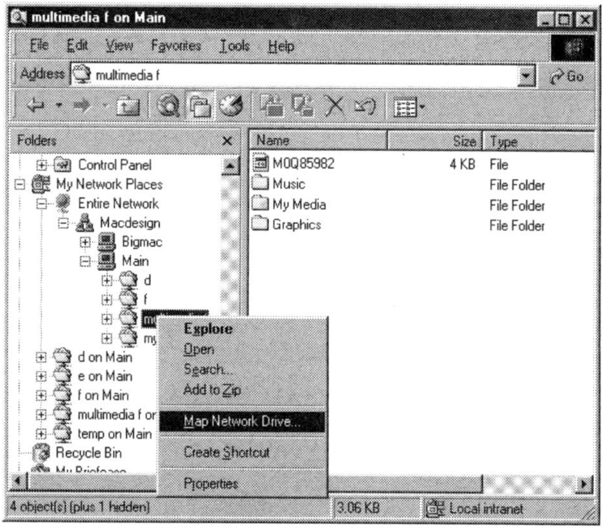

3 The next unused drive letter will be offered – change it only if you need to.

4 If you always need to map this drive, tick **Reconnect at logon** to save having to do this again.

5 Click **OK**.

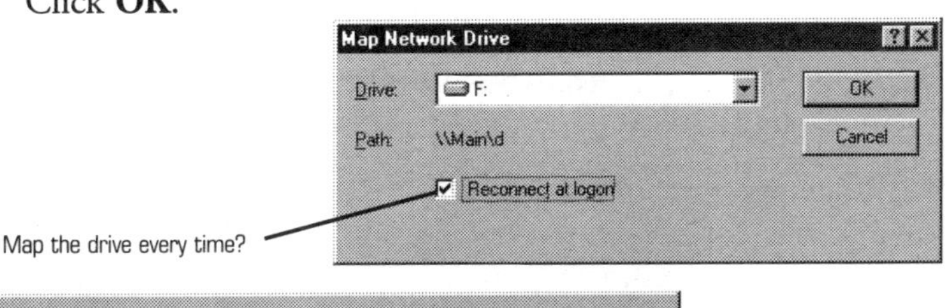

Map the drive every time?

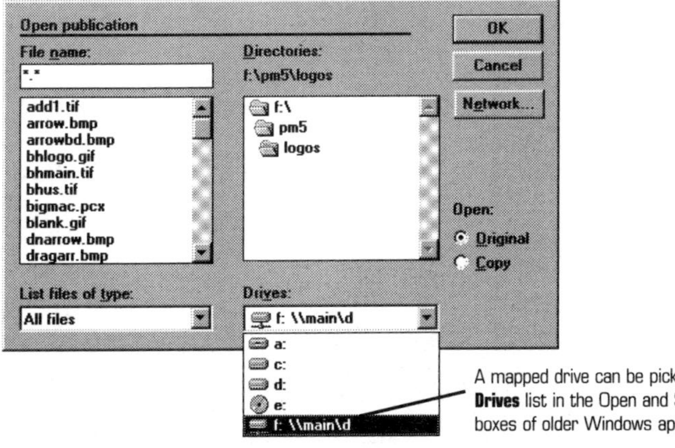

A mapped drive can be picked from the **Drives** list in the Open and Save dialog boxes of older Windows applications

Share an Internet connection

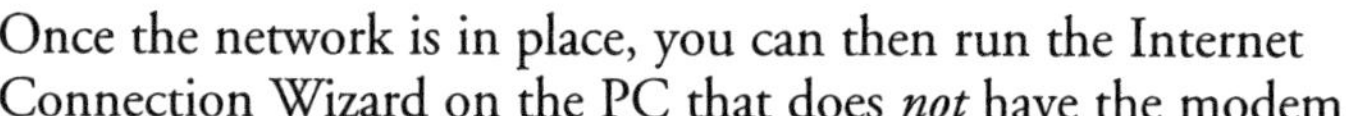

Once the network is in place, you can then run the Internet Connection Wizard on the PC that does *not* have the modem.

You will find the Wizard in the **Programs → Accessories → Communications** menu. It is simple to use.

- At the first panels, tell it you want to set up the connection manually and through a LAN (Local Area Network).
- When you reach the stage shown opposite, select **Automatic discovery of proxy server** and let the Wizard sort it out. The PC with the modem is acting as a *proxy server* – one making the connection for another. Don't try to configure it yourself – that option is there for special situations and keen techies.
- If you have not yet set up the PC for e-mail, you will need to have details of your e-mail account to hand – your user name, the name of your mail server and whether it is a POP3, IMAP or HTTP server. If you do not know, ask your ISP.

tip

The connection is fully shared. Not only can all the networked PCs use the connection, they can use it at the same time.

Leave it to the Wizard

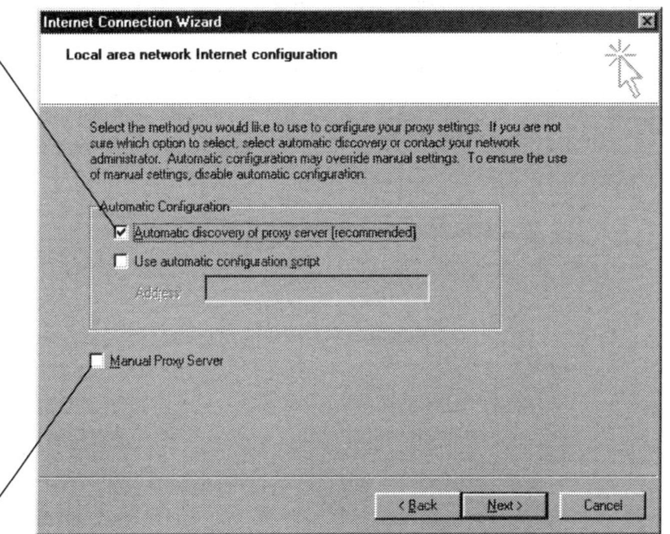

Don't try this at home!

tip

Internet connection sharing may not work with some ISPs. If you have problems, check that they can handle it.

ACCESSORIES

Text and images

Discover WordPad

Don't underrate WordPad just because it's free. It's fine for writing letters, essays, reports and anything else where you want to be able to edit text efficiently, formatting it with fonts, styles and colours, and perhaps incorporating graphics or other files.

- When entering text, just keep typing when you reach the edge of the page – the text will be wrapped round to the next line. Only press the **Enter** key at the end of a paragraph.
- Most formatting can be done through the toolbar. Select the text, then pick a font or size from the drop-down lists, or click the B bold, I italic, U underline, or other buttons.
- The left, centre and right alignment buttons determine how the text lines up with the edges of the paper.

tip

The techniques you learn with WordPad can be applied to Word and most other word-processors.

- The bullets button indents text from the left, with a blob at the start of each paragraph.
- Alignment and bullet formats apply to whole paragraphs. A paragraph is selected if the cursor is within it, or if any part of the paragraph is selected.

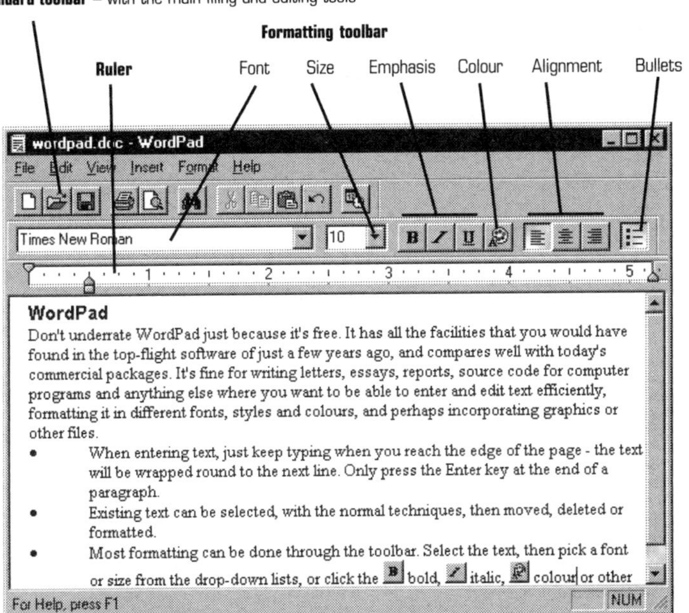

Set indents and tabs

Indents push the text in from the page margins. The first line of a paragraph can – and often is – indented less or more than the rest of the text.

Tabs are used to line up text in columns. In WordPad there are only *left* tabs – these align the columns of text by their left sides.

- To set the indents, select the text to be indented then drag their markers as required.
- To set tabs, select the text to which they will apply then click on the ruler to create a new tab, or drag an existing one to a new place.

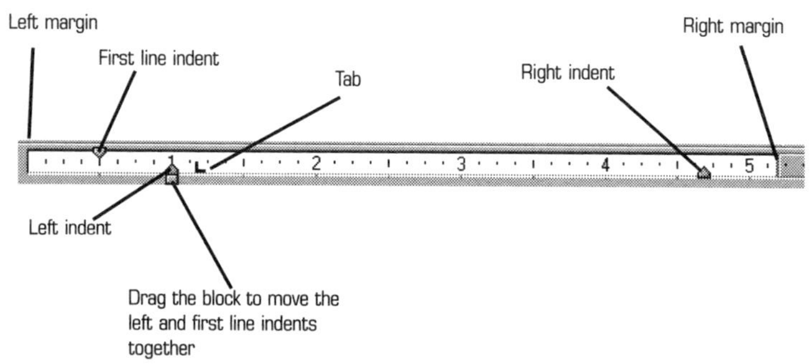

Format fonts

You can set most font options from the toolbar buttons, but you get better control through the **Font** dialog box. Here you can set all aspects of a font, and preview the effects of your choices.

1 Select the text to be formatted.

2 Open the dialog box with **Format → Font**.

3 Work through the options to define the font – watch the **Sample** text as you change the settings.

4 Click **OK**.

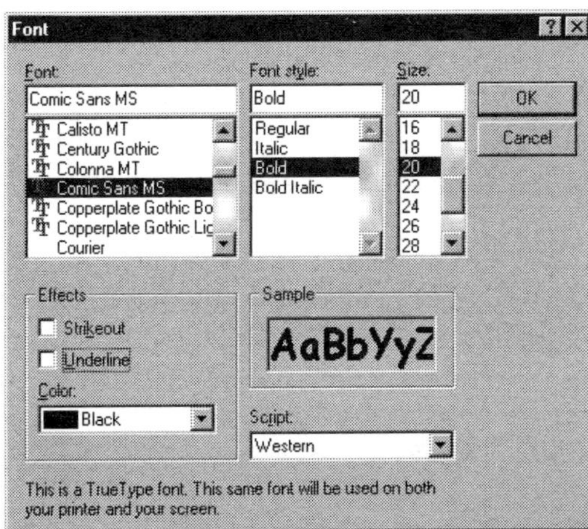

You will find similar panels in all applications that use fonts

Define the Page Setup

The **Page Setup** panel, opened from the **File** menu option, controls the basic size and layout of the page – for all pages in the document.

- The **Paper Size** and **Source** settings rarely need changing – if you've set your printer properties correctly. If you are printing on card or special paper, change the **Source** to *Manual*, if the option is available.
- In the **Orientation** area, *Portrait* is the normal way up; use *Landscape* if you want to print with the paper sideways.
- The **Margins** set the overall limits to the printable area. You can use the indents to reduce the width of text within the margins, but you cannot extend out beyond them.
- Click the **Printer** button to reach its **Properties** panel to change any settings at that level – you might, for example, want to switch to a lower resolution for printing a draft copy, or a higher resolution for the final output. (See pages 150 to 163 for more on printers.)

THE **PAGE SETUP** PANEL IN WORDPAD

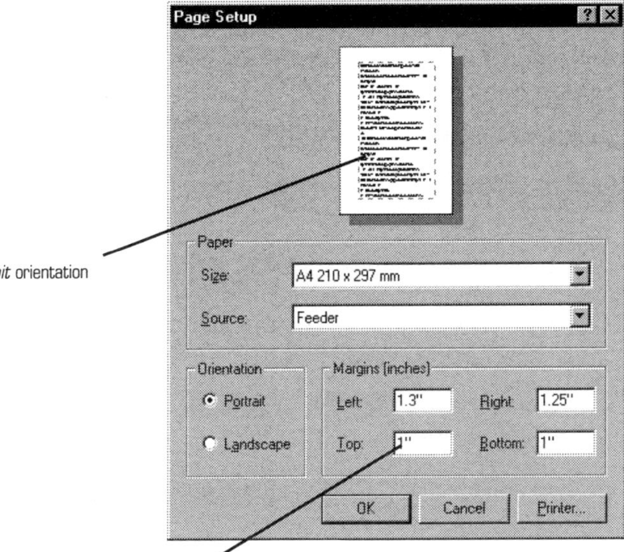

This is *Portrait* orientation

Measurements here are in inches, but can be changed on the **Options** panel that opens from the **View** menu

Insert graphics and other objects

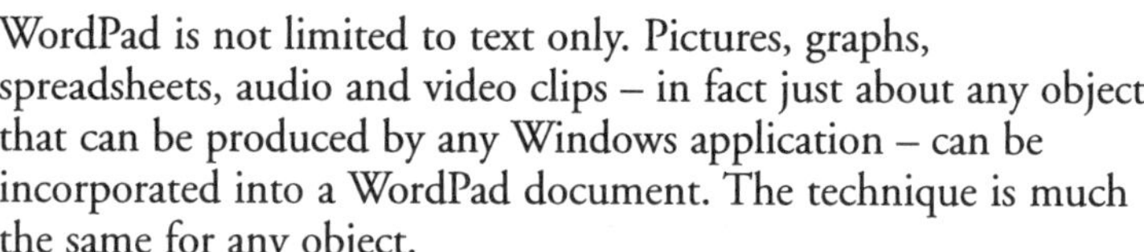

WordPad is not limited to text only. Pictures, graphs, spreadsheets, audio and video clips – in fact just about any object that can be produced by any Windows application – can be incorporated into a WordPad document. The technique is much the same for any object.

1 Open the **Insert** menu and select **Object...**

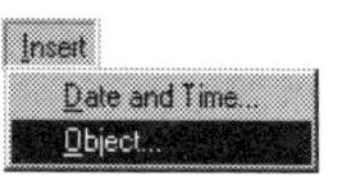

2 If the object does not yet exist, select **Create New** and pick the **Object Type**, then click **OK**.

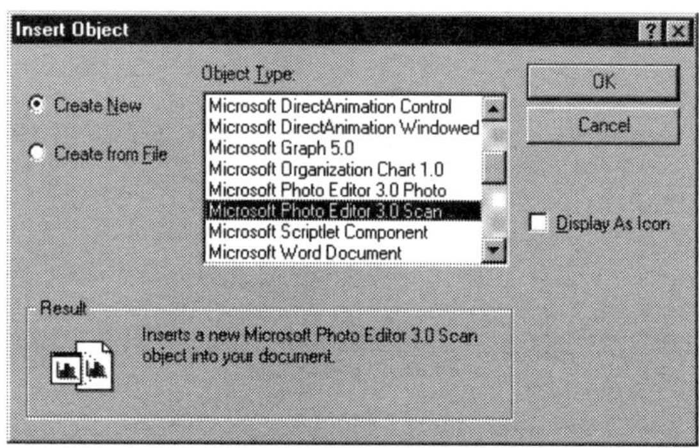

The application will open. When you have created the object, save it if you want to keep a copy for future use, then select the new **Exit & Return to Document** option from its **File** menu.

3 If you want to use an existing object, select **Create from File**, and browse through your folders to locate it.

4 Back in your WordPad document, you can resize the object if necessary.

The position of the object across the page can be set using the alignment buttons

Select the object – it will be outlined with handles at the corners and mid-edges

Point to a handle to get the double-headed arrow then drag in or out as required

ADJUSTING THE SIZE OF AN IMAGE IN WORDPAD. AN INSERTED OBJECT CAN BE EDITED BY DOUBLE-CLICKING ON IT – THIS OPENS THE SOURCE APPLICATION. USE EXIT & RETURN WHEN YOU HAVE FINISHED EDITING

Preview before printing

Most applications have a Print Preview facility, and it is always useful, as it can be difficult to tell how a document will look on paper. Use the Preview to get a better idea of the final output, before you print. Do the images and headings have the impact that you want? Do you get bad breaks in the text at the ends of pages? If it looks good, you can print from here by clicking **Print**, if not, click **Close** to return to WordPad for that final tweaking.

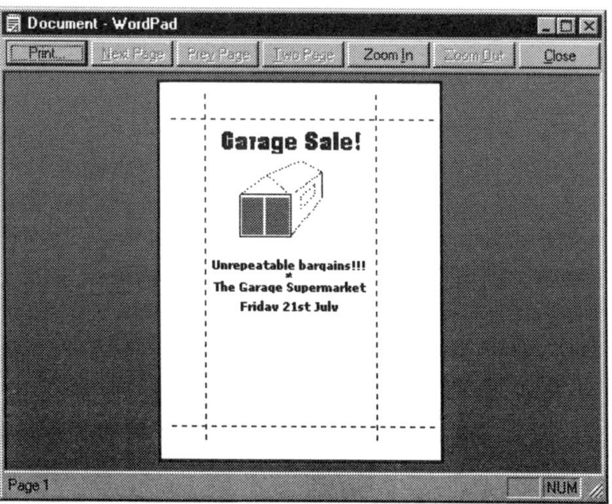

USE THE PRINT PREVIEW TO CHECK THE LAYOUT. YOU CAN PRINT FROM HERE, OR CLOSE TO RETURN TO EDITING

Save a file

In WordPad as in all applications you should save early and save often! Don't wait until you have finished writing that eight-page report before you save it. Applications can crash, hardware can fail, plugs get knocked out and we all make mistakes! The first save may take a few moments, but later saves are done at the click of a button.

To save a file for the first time:

1 Open the **File** menu and select **Save As...**

2 At the dialog box, select the folder.

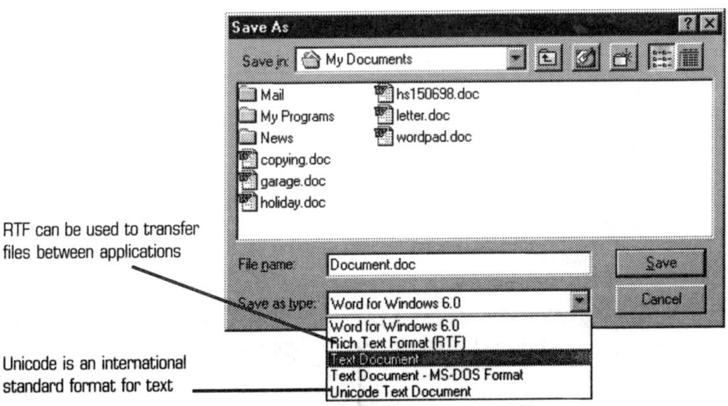

3 Change the default *Document* in the filename to something that will remind you what it is about.

4 If you want to save in a different format, pick one from the **Save as type** drop-down list.

5 Click **Save**.

To resave the current document:

- Click [save icon] – that's it!

When you close the document, or exit from WordPad, if you have not saved the document in its final state, you will be prompted to do so.

tip

If you use WordPad to create HTML documents (Web pages) or the source code for programs, you'll save the file as Text. WordPad will automatically add *.txt* to the end of the filename – which is not wanted! For example, the Web page that you wanted to call *mypage.htm* will be saved as *mypage.htm.txt*. After you exit WordPad, find the file in My Computer and edit the filename to get rid of the extra extension.

Open a file

Next time that you want to work on the document, open it from the **File** menu. Either:

- Select **Open** and then browse for the file – the dialog box is used in almost exactly the same way as the Save dialog box.

Or

- If it is one of the files that you have used most recently, it will be listed at the bottom of the **File** menu. Select it from here.

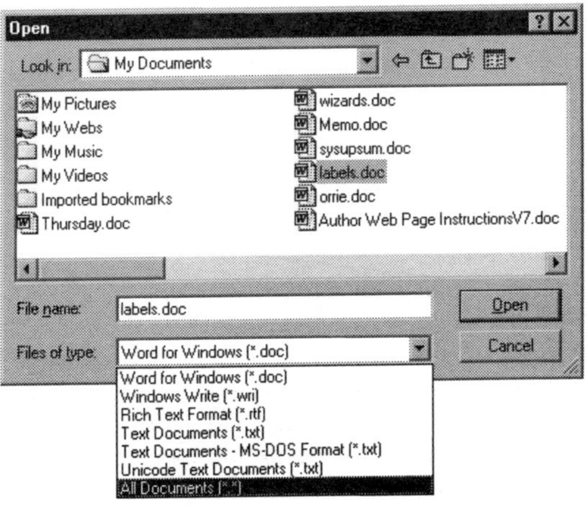

Use the Character Map

You will find **Character Map** on the **System Tools** menu – don't ask me why! It's a useful tool and one that I like to have close to hand. It allows you to see the characters available in any font, and to copy individual characters from there into a document.

Next time that you want a symbol, accented letter or other unusual character in any document, use the Map.

1 From the **Start** menu, go to the **Programs → Accessories → System Tools** menu and select the **Character Map**.

2 Pick a font from the drop-down list – Symbol, Webdings and Wingdings are the main fonts for decorative characters, and you will find foreign letters and mathematical symbols in most other fonts.

3 Hold down the left button and move across the display – the character under the cursor will be enlarged.

4 To copy characters into a document, click **Select** – the current one will be added to the **Characters to copy** display – then click Copy when you have all you want. Return to your document and use **Edit → Paste** – the character(s) will be copied in, formatted to the chosen font.

Or

5 Make a note of the **Keystroke** in the bottom right corner. If it says **Alt+…** you can get that character by holding down **Alt** and typing the numbers (with the leading 0) into the *Number keypad*.

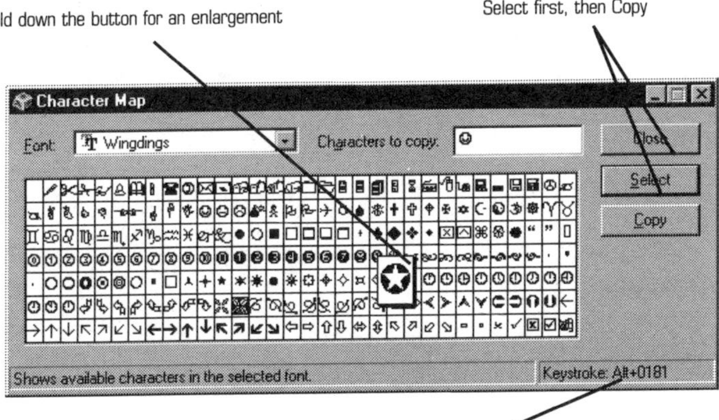

If you are likely to want to use a character regularly, make a note of its Keystroke

Remember that the appearance of the character depends upon the font.

Dabble with Paint

Graphics software falls into two broad groups. With some, including **Paint**, the image is produced by applying colour to a background – with each new line overwriting anything that may be beneath. Using these is very like real painting. You may be able to wipe out a mistake while the paint is still wet, but as soon as it has dried it is fixed on the canvas. (Paint allows you to undo the last move; some will let you backtrack further.)

The second type works with objects – lines, circles, text notes, etc. – that remain separate, and can be moved, deleted, recoloured and otherwise changed at any point. **Imaging** works this way (see page 230).

I use Paint regularly – it's ideal for trimming and tidying screenshots for books, though I don't expect many of you will want it for this purpose. Though it can be used to produce intricate images, these require a great deal of time and skill – and can be created more successfully on a computer art package, with a full set of shading, shaping and manipulating tools. Paint is probably best used to draw simple diagrams, or to get an idea of how this type of graphics software works.

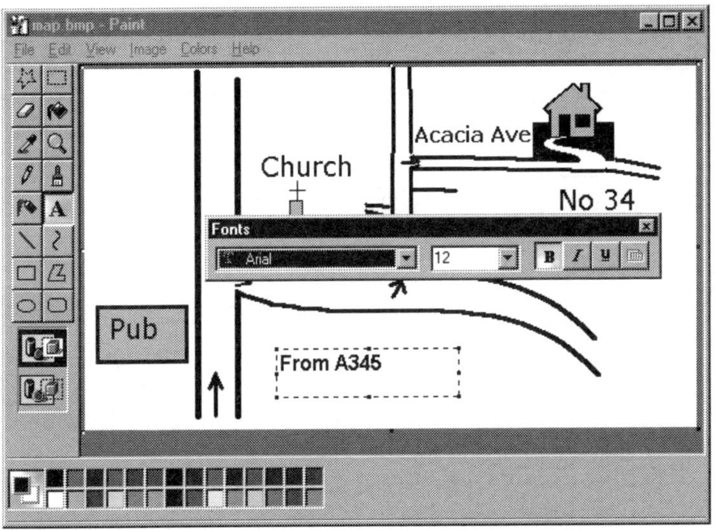

USING PAINT TO CREATE A DIAGRAM. THE TEXT TOOLBAR GIVES YOU THE FULL RANGE OF FONTS AND THE MAIN STYLE EFFECTS

The Toolbox

There is a simple but adequate set of tools.

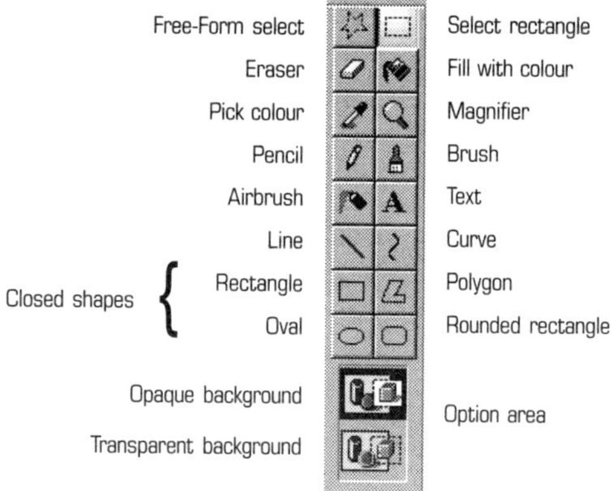

A little experimentation will show how they all work, but note these points:

- The *Pencil*, *Brush* and *Airbrush* lay down the foreground colour when the left button is held down, and the background colour when the right button is pressed.
- With the *Line* and the closed shapes, click where you want one end of the line or corner of the shape to be, then drag to the opposite end/corner.

- *Pick colour* is used to select a colour off the screen – press the right button to use it to select a background colour.
- If you hold down the right button when using the *Eraser*, it will replace anything in the foreground colour with the background colour, without affecting anything else.

Most of the tools have options that can be set in the area below the toolbar.

- When you select an area (or paste an image from a file or from the Clipboard) the background can be transparent or opaque.
- You can set the size of the *Eraser*, *Brush*, *Airbrush*, *Line* and *Curve*. N.B. the Line thickness applies to the closed shapes.
- The *Magnifier* is 4× by default, but can be 2×, 6× or 8×.
- The *Pencil* is only ever 1 pixel wide.
- *Closed shapes* can be outline or fill only, or both.

Work with selected areas

The rectangular and free-form selectors can be used to select an area of the screen.

1 To select a regular area, use the *Rectangle select* tool. Click at the top left of the area and drag to the opposite corner – a dashed frame indicates the area being selected.

2 To select an irregular area, use the *Freeform select* tool. Drag an outline around the area – it'll probably be wobbly, but as long as it selects the right bit, why worry?

3 Once selected, an area can be:

- *Deleted* – which can be a neater way to remove excess bits than using the eraser.
- *Copied* – handy for creating repeating patterns.
- *Saved as a file* – use **Edit → Copy To...** and give a filename.
- *Dragged elsewhere* on screen.
- *Flipped* (mirrored) horizontally or vertically, or rotated in 90° increments – use **Image → Flip/Rotate** for these effects.
- *Stretched* – to enlarge, shrink or distort; or *skewed*, either horizontally or vertically – use **Image → Stretch/Skew**.

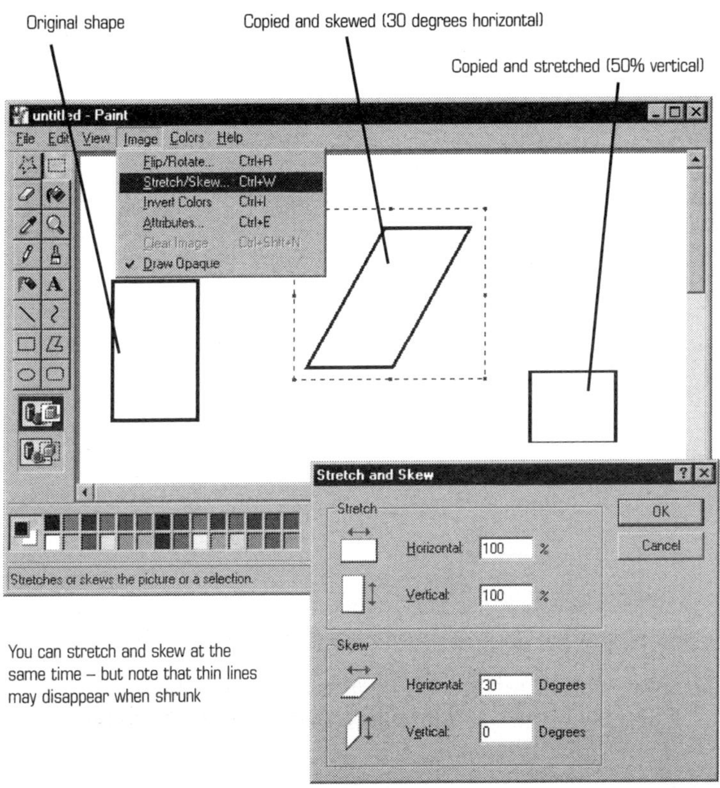

You can stretch and skew at the same time – but note that thin lines may disappear when shrunk

Select and mix colours

The colour palette is used in much the same way in all Windows programs. You can select a colour – use the left button for the foreground and the right for the background – or mix your own.

To define a colour:

1 Double-click on a colour in the **Color Box** or use **Colors → Edit Colors** to open the **Edit Colors** panel.

2 Initially only the **Basic colors** will be visible. Click **Define Custom Colors** to open the full panel.

3 Drag the cross-hair cursor in the main square to set the Red/Green/Blue balance, and move the arrow up or down the left scale to set the light/dark level.

4 Colours can also be set by typing in values, but note that you are mixing light, not paint.

- Red and green make yellow;
- Red, green and blue make grey/white;
- The more you use, the lighter the colour.

5 When you have the colour you want, click **Add to Custom Colors**. The new colour will replace the one currently selected in the Color Box on the main screen.

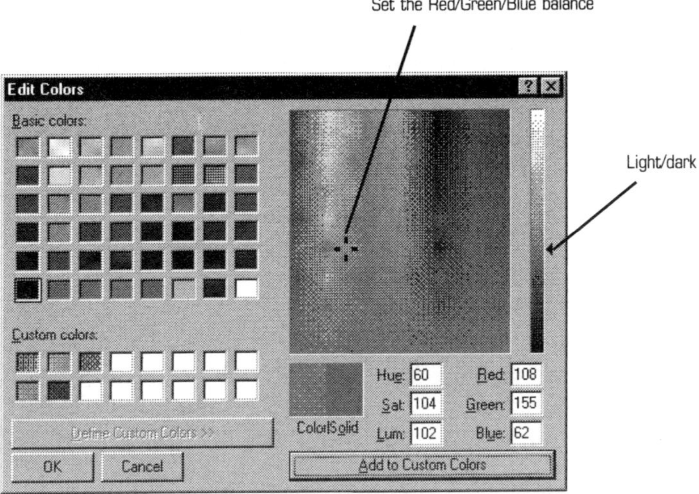

tip

If you press the **Prt Sc** (Print Screen) key, the whole screen is copied into the Clipboard. If you press **Alt** + **Prt Sc** then only the active window is copied. The image can be pasted into Paint, or any other graphics program, and saved from there. That's how the screenshots were produced for this book.

Draw a curve in Paint

The *Curve* is probably the trickiest of the tools to use. The line can have one or two curves to it.

1 Draw a line between the points where the curve will start and end.

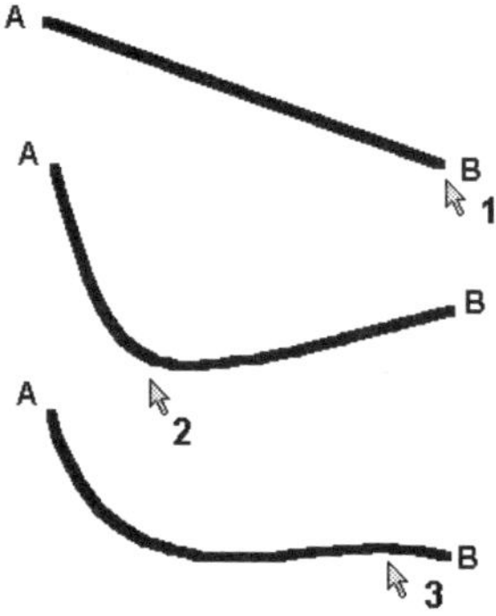

2 Drag to create the first curve – exaggerate the curve as it will normally be reduced at the next stage.

3 If the line is to have a second curve, drag it out now – as long as the mouse button is down, the line will flex to follow the cursor.

4 For a simple curve, just click at the end of the line.

tip

If you go wrong any time – and you will with the Curve – use **Edit → Undo**. This removes the effect of the last action.

Save or open a picture file

A normal Save will save the whole working area, in 24-bit (high colour) bitmap format. These are large files. Files will be smaller if you save with fewer colours or in the (256 colour) GIF format.

- You can also use **Edit → Copy To...** to save a selected part of an image as a separate file.

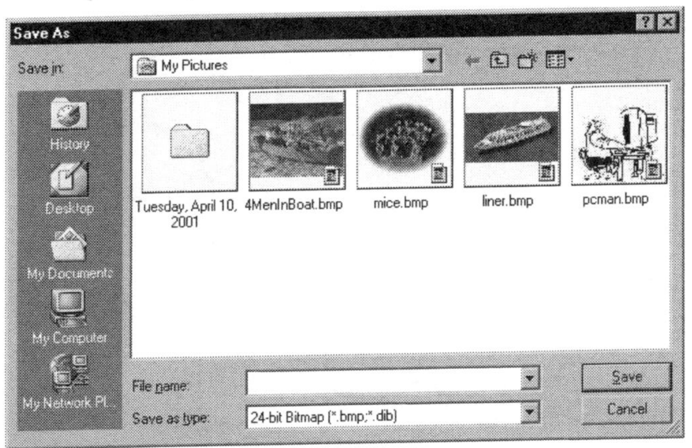

tip

You can use **Edit → Paste From...** to merge a file into a picture.

Edit images with Imaging

You can use **Imaging** to take images in from a scanner or a file and add simple annotations to them. Text can be added on a transparent background, or as a stick-on note. There are drawing tools for freehand or straight lines, and filled or open rectangles – enough for simple diagrams, but nothing much more!

Notes and drawn objects can be selected and edited at any point

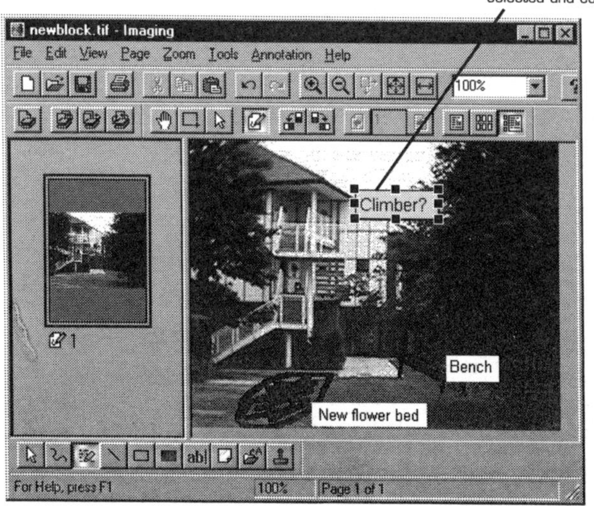

USING IMAGING TO ANNOTATE A SCANNED PICTURE. THE SCREEN IS SEEN HERE IN **PAGE AND THUMBNAIL VIEW**. SWITCH TO **PAGE VIEW** AND INCREASE THE ZOOM LEVEL FOR CLOSE-UP WORK

One of the interesting aspects of this program is the way that the image is formed. Each note, line or rectangle is a separate object. You can click on it at any point and move, resize or delete it, or change its colour, font or thickness.

When you use a tool, the object that you create will be in the default colour, thickness and font. These can be changed by right-clicking on the object and selecting **Properties** from the shortcut menu. The defaults for a tool can be changed by right-clicking on its button and opening its **Properties** panel – well worth doing if you want to use the same tool several times with the same effects.

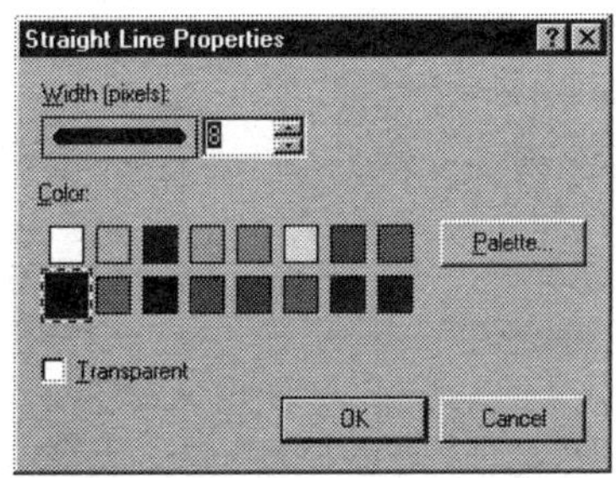

Imaging has a few, limited editing facilities: you can cut, copy and paste rectangular areas, and the whole image can be rotated.

On the positive side, Imaging can read images in most major formats and can save as TIFF files (a high quality and very portable format, handled by many applications), as BMPs (like Paint) and AWD (fax format). You can use it to create multi-page documents, and these can be printed, faxed or e-mailed.

Utilities and media

Calculator

Pack away that pocket calculator. You don't need it on your desk now that you have one on your Desktop!

The Calculator can work in two modes – Standard or Scientific. In either case, you use it in the same way that you would a hand-held calculator. Enter the numbers, arithmetic operators and functions either by clicking on the screen keys, or by using your keyboard. (If you want to use the keyboard in the Scientific mode, look in the Help file for the keyboard equivalents.)

It has the same limitations as a simple pocket calculator – you can only store one value in memory at a time (**MS** to store it, **M+** to add to the value in memory, **MR** to recall it and **MC** to clear it); and you cannot print your results. If you want more than this, use a spreadsheet!

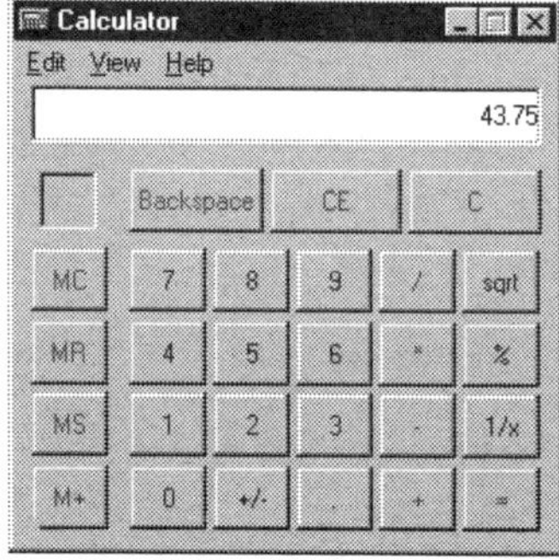

Phone Dialer

Phone Dialer is on the **Programs → Accessories → Communications** menu. To use it, you must have your modem plugged into the phone line. To use it conveniently, you should have a phone on your desk.

You can dial a number here, rather than on the phone, but that's not worth doing unless the phone keypad is out of reach.

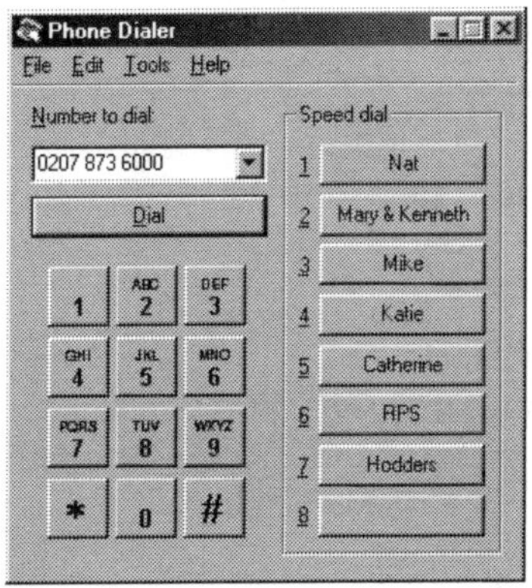

The real benefit of Phone Dialer is in the **Speed dial** facility, which can act as an extension to, or in place of, any memory buttons on the phone. (Setting up and changing Speed dial numbers here is far simpler than on my phone!) Up to 8 numbers can be stored.

Set up a Speed dial number

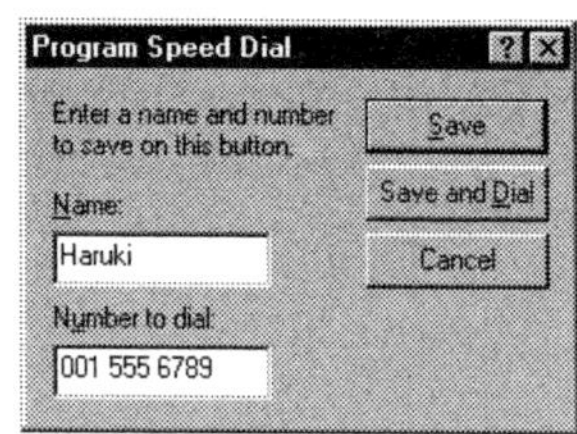

1 Click on an unused Speed dial button.

2 Enter the **Name** and **Number**.

3 Click **Save**, or **Save and Dial** if you want to call immediately.

To edit a number:

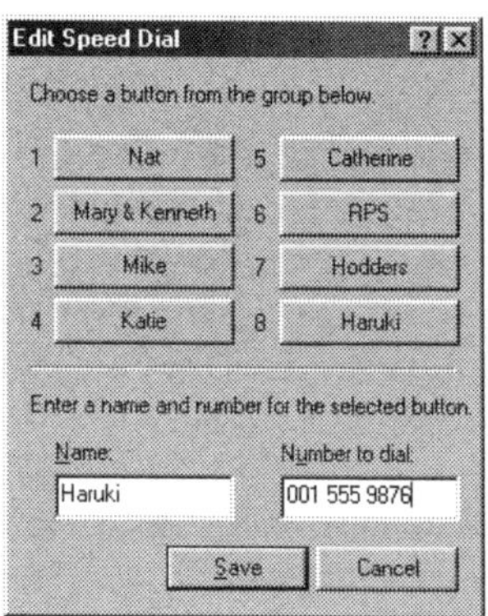

1 Open the **Edit** menu and select **Speed Dial...**

2 Click on the button.

3 Edit and click **Save**.

- New numbers can be set up here – click a blank button to start.

To make a Speed Dial call:

1 Click on the button.

2 When you get through, click **Talk** at the prompt.

3 When you have done, click **Hang up**.

Media Player

Media Player is a multi-purpose audio/video player. It can handle sound files in MIDI and in the native Windows format, WAVE, audio CDs, and video in the Video for Windows (AVI), Media Audio/Video (WMA and ASF) or ActiveMovie formats.

Video

Newer, faster hardware and more efficient software have significantly improved the quality of videos on PC, but they are still grainy and jerky. The main sources of videos are multimedia packages, demos and samples on CDs, and the Internet.

There are three main ways to get video from the Internet:

- Clips for downloading – the new high-compression formats have brought a better balance between download time and playing time. 1Mb of video gives you around 90 seconds of playing time, and will take up to 10 minutes to download.
- *Streaming* video in TV and webcam broadcasts and in movie and pop video clips. Here the videos are played as they download. The images are jerkier, but at least you don't have to wait to see whether they are worth watching at all.
- Home movies e-mailed to you by relatives, who have been playing with Movie Maker (see page 243).

Play a CD Audio

Want some music while you work? Let Media Player play a CD for you.

1 Load in the CD and wait for Media Player to start and to read in the track information.

- The CD will play in the tracks in their playlist sequence – initially this will be the standard order.

2 To change the order of tracks, click on one to select it, then drag up or down.

3 To skip over tracks, select them, then right-click and choose **Disable** from the shortcut menu.

tip

It's worth taking time over organizing the playlist, as the information that you enter is stored in a file on the hard disk and will be reused next time the same CD is loaded.

Media Player may struggle with the last tracks on long CDs.

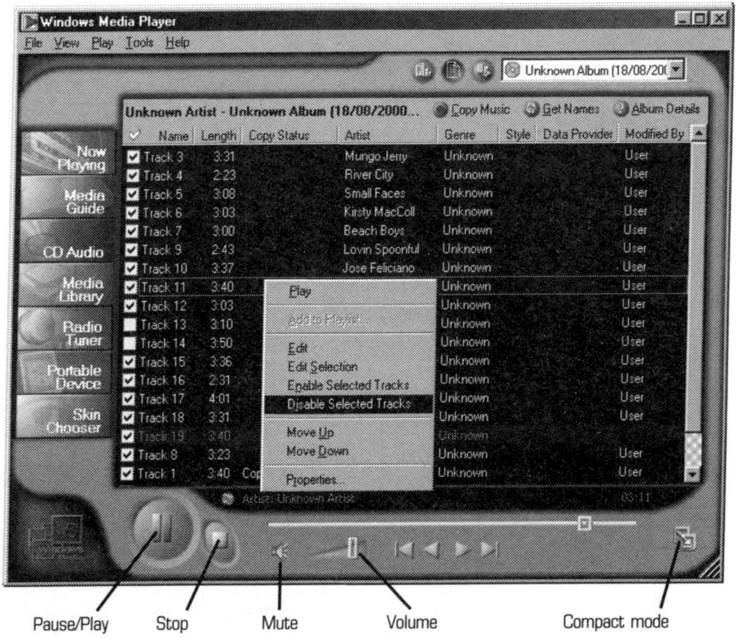

Pause/Play Stop Mute Volume Compact mode

MEDIA PLAYER, SHOWING THE PLAYLIST FOR AN AUDIO CD

Listen to the radio

The **Radio Tuner** offers another way to get to the same Internet radio stations that you can reach through the Radio toolbar in Internet Explorer.

1 Go online.

2 Open **Media Player** and click the **Radio Tuner** button.

3 Media Player will link to **media.com**. On the left, you will see a list of a dozen pre-set stations, catering to a range of tastes – pick a station, or…

4 In the **Station Finder**, pick *Format* in the first drop-down list, and a type from the second, then choose a station. (You can also list by language or place, or search by call sign, frequency or keyword – there are hundreds of stations.)

5 Internet Explorer will normally open to show you the station's Web site. This can be closed down if not wanted, to save screen space and speed up download of the broadcast.

Obviously, if you are paying for your phone time when you are online, this is not an efficient way to listen to the radio!

The reception is not brilliant – expect some gaps and crackles – but can you pick up stations in the USA, Australia, Italy, Vietnam, etc. on your Hi Fi?

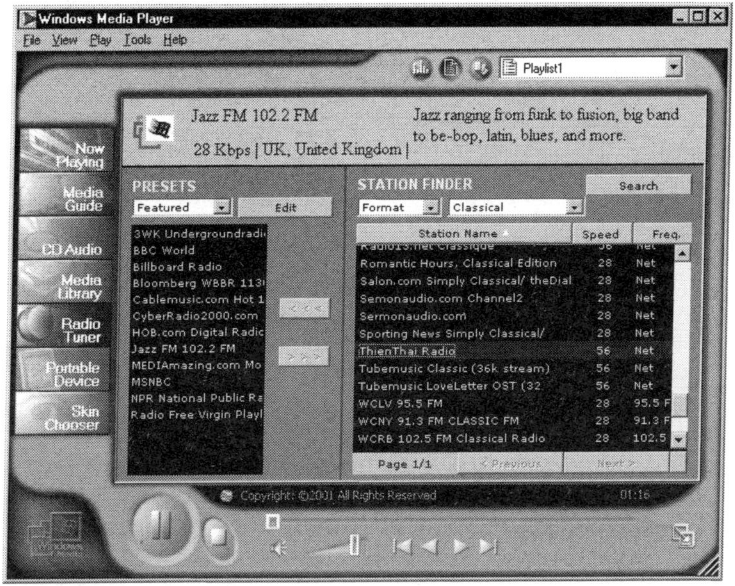

LISTENING TO JAZZ FM, WHILE LOOKING TO SEE WHAT STATIONS OFFER CLASSICAL MUSIC – THERE ARE DOZENS. HOW DO I CHOOSE ONE?!

Choose a skin

Once the playlist is set up and the CD is playing, you can switch into compact mode. This doesn't just occupy less screen space; it also has some great 'skins', which vary from the sublime to the ridiculous (I like this one, it's jolly!)

To choose and use a skin:

1 Click the **Skin Chooser** button.

2 Click on a skin in the list and click **Apply Skin**.

3 To restore the full display, click – this is hard to spot on some skins.

If a skin has a screen, a 'visualization' will run in it while music is playing. If you want to change this, open the **View** menu, point to **Visualization**, select a set then pick one from there. None seem to respond much to changes in rhythm, pitch or volume, so don't expect a *son et lumière* experience.

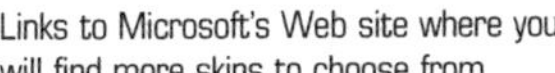

Links to Microsoft's Web site where you will find more skins to choose from

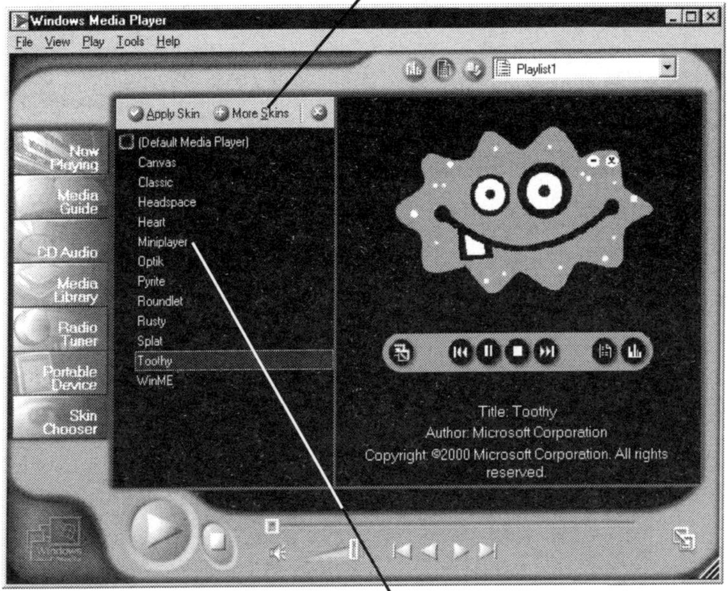

A skin is a more compact display than the full player – and if compactness is the main reason for using a skin, choose *Miniplayer*

Manage your music

Media Player's other tabs allow you to manage your music (and video) in different ways.

Media Guide

This links to Microsoft's Media Guide site, from where you can download samples, clips and much more. Have a browse next time you are online.

Media Library

Use this to organize the audio and video files currently on your PC. You can list audio files by album, artist or genre, and video files by author. Having located a file, double-click on it to run it.

Portable Device

If you own a pocket or palm-size PC, you can use this facility to copy files from your hard drive, or from an audio CD onto the device.

Movie Maker

You can use this to edit digital video, taking images in directly from your camera. The video is automatically split into clips, which can then be split further or trimmed and set into a new sequence. You can merge in other video clips, or add still images, for titles and credits, or a voice-over or background music. Altogether, this is quite a competent editing suite. If you have the time and the skill, you can produce some good movies.

The Movie Maker format takes around 10Kb for each second of playing time. This means that video files are not small, though they are very much more compact than the ones produced by older formats, and sharing them with distant friends and relatives via the Internet is now quite feasible.

There are two ways to do it:

- Send the movie by e-mail. Files are increased in size by 50% when attached to a message (it's to do with the way that data is transferred through the mail system), but you can normally download e-mail at 3Kb or more per second.
- Upload the file to your home page, and just send the URL to people. There are two catches to this: you have to have at least a basic grasp of putting home pages together, and download times from the Web are typically less than 2Kb per second.

What it boils down to is that it is going to take your friends and relatives around one minute to download 100Kb of video, which will play for 10 seconds. That 10 minute video of the little one's birthday party will take over an hour to get, but if they are on the other side of the world, it may be an hour well spent.

The clips can be trimmed and rearranged freely

PLAYING WITH THE SAMPLE FILE IN MOVIE MAKER. I DON'T THINK I'VE GOT A FUTURE IN MOVIES – YOU MAY HAVE!

Notes

Notes